How Are You Feeling, Momma? (You ... me at its subtitle. As women—and es... pressure to be fine…or seem fine…or say "I'm fine" always feels like it's hovering over our interactions. But as God speaks to us through the Psalms, He clearly gives us permission to express the full range of emotions He intentionally equipped us with when He created us! I love that Lisa and Shelby's book takes firm hold of this divine go-ahead and expands on it with an accessible "What am I feeling now?" emotional buffet. However you're feeling at the moment, Momma—from afraid to worshipful to something in between—you're not alone, and this reassuring resource offers proof of that from two beautiful moms who aren't willing to settle for "I'm fine" and don't think you should either.

- Elizabeth Spencer, mom of one teen and one 20-something daughter. Blogs at guiltychocoholicmama.blogspot.com

As a mother of six, reading *How are You Feeling, Momma?* is like sitting on my front porch with a couple of friends and having a much-needed conversation.

- Laura Wolf, mom of six, ages 10 and under

This book is a delightful guide for mothers and grandmothers to reflect on the spiritual joys & challenges of motherhood. I enjoyed the two different perspectives, which bring alive the love of God through all the turmoil of motherhood and the world.

- Sandy McLeod, mom of two, grandmother of three

Whether we identify as Jewish or Christian, as moms, when we open Scripture, we're reading the same Psalms. It's a beautiful thing to realize, as these women did, the way we apply the truths we read, in our home lives, our communities, and in our places of worship, are remarkably similar too.

- Traci Rhoades, mom of one 11-year-old. Blogs at tracesoffaith.com

How Are You Feeling, Momma?

(You don't need to say, "I'm fine.")

Authentic & Encouraging Psalm Reflections on the Many Emotions of Motherhood

SHELBY SPEAR, Jesus Groupie
LISA LESHAW, Moses Devotee

Two Moms, Two Faiths, Two Voices

How Are You Feeling, Momma?
(You don't need to say, "I'm fine.")

ISBN-13: 978-0-578-42418-7
Ebook ISBN: 978-0-578-44907-4

Library of Congress Cataloging-in-Publication Data (to come)
Printed in the United States of America

Cover design by TC Schwindling
Editing/developmental editing/copyediting by Jana Burson
Proofreading by Andi Pitman

Lisa Leshaw is an ultra-liberal, Jewish, New York step-mom joining forces with a pro-love, Jesus-adoring, Ohio mom, Shelby Spear. On paper, these two would appear to be polar opposites. Ironically, their differences are the adhesive that binds them in this joint effort to give moms some spiritual uplift while in the trenches of motherhood. A serendipitous online encounter brought them together, and these two are living proof that despite differing views, backgrounds, and cultures, when it comes to God, all things are possible through love.

Contents

Acknowledgments

To my hubby and best friend, John, whose selfless love, sacrifice, and service to our family created the opportunity for me to nurture our kids from inside the nest and work toward my dreams in the process. For my three precious kiddos—utmost models of love, compassion, and grace—who made me the woman I am today.

~Shelby

No one believes in me or puts up with me more than the Mister, so thank you, Stu Leshaw. You're a glorious partner and the perfect anchor to my kite. And to my kids, who are the root of my gray hair and who constantly melt my soul, I could not be more proud of you. And to Leslie Means and the Glorious Warriors from Her View From Home, your gifts transform women's lives. Mine Included.
God Bless. WRITE ON

~ Lisa

Foreword

Every mother will experience a plethora of emotions during her parenting journey. This extraordinary road we travel can be filled with an abundance of joy as we raise our children through all the ages and stages and phases of growth. But amidst the joy, there are also moments of feeling deep angst, fear, loneliness, sadness, discouragement, frustration, confusion, guilt, shame, and utter overwhelm that grabs hold of our momma hearts.

Although every mom will travel down a unique parenting road, there are common issues we all face, challenges we all encounter, and struggles we all endure. Being a momma is hard. The unpredictable roller-coaster ride full of emotional twists and turns and highs and lows can leave us depleted and defeated.

Talking about those raw and very real emotions can be uncomfortable and embarrassing. We may be fearful of judgment or rejection if we expose our true selves. And oftentimes, moms just don't have the energy to be vulnerable when we are constantly running in the relentless race of mothering.

So, when people ask how we're doing or how we're feeling, we often respond with a casual *"I'm fine."* It's just easier not to go *'there.'*

But how do we manage those deep emotions that come from raising our kids? How do we best take care of ourselves? What do we do with those aches that come with motherhood?

I believe the greatest relief and the most powerful affirmation comes from connection. There is a universal bond moms experience, created through a mutual understanding of our profound love and a fierce passion for our children. When moms can have intimate and honest conversations with other trusted moms about how they are really feeling, restoration occurs.

It's in this book where you will find freedom from hiding, from holding in those true emotions, from having to keep it all together with a perfectly coined "I'm fine." You can be real here. You can be you. You can reveal those sensitive parts and secret struggles as you realize you are not alone.

Shelby Spear and Lisa Leshaw have combined their writing gifts, their two walks of faith, and their generous love for helping moms to offer you much-needed nourishment through helpful advice, inspiring Biblical truths, and an intimate view into their own well-worn experience as mothers.

Soak it all in, dear moms. Each chapter will drench you in the grace poured from these pages and tend to those fragile pieces of your heart that need to be handled with utmost care. You will find revelation, redemption, and a refreshing dose of faithful inspiration as these two seasoned moms meet you exactly where you're at and offer you the wisdom and encouragement you need.

Remember that you were designed by the hands of a loving God for this mission of motherhood. He goes before you and prepares the way. He walks this glorious and exhausting road alongside you with His unfailing love.

Let Shelby and Lisa speak truth into your lives, blanket you with comforting reassurance, and spur you on with fortitude and faith.

Christine Carter
Mom of two teens ages 13 and 15, and author of *Help and Hope While You're Healing: A woman's guide toward wellness while recovering from injury, surgery, or illness. Blogs at themomcafe.com*

Introduction

A Note from Shelby

The simple question, "How are you feeling, Momma?" wins the prize for the most loaded inquiry in the history of all things wonder. As moms, we've concocted a gazillion ways to dodge and deflect the question in order to avoid giving an honest answer. A trite *"I'm fine"* keeps the heaviness of authenticity from mucking up our everyday living.

Yet, the truth is, beneath our facade are countless felt needs just begging for healing and resolve. Motherhood is full of competing emotions that sap our energy on the regular. We often choose to ignore our feelings because if we give them room to breathe, scary things can happen. One of which is a complete unraveling of all the 'fake it until you make it' holding us together. Who wants to risk coming undone when we're already on 'overwhelmed mother' status? But trying to side-step our reality by not being genuine only adds to the emotional weight we carry because of the missed opportunities to unburden our heart.

The good news is God is ready and willing to listen to how we feel. He already knows our heart anyway. His presence never leaves us, which means the availability God has on any given day to hear our prayers, pleadings, worries, and fears is all of time and eternity.

Seems like the Hebrews took full advantage of this truth back in the day when you consider the Psalms. Turns out all the *"Why, God?", "Why not, God?", "When, God?", "How, God?", and "*Are *you* *sure, God?"* questions hanging in the air thousands of years ago still resonate in our heart space today.

The Psalms depict what the Hebrews felt at the heart level as opposed to other writings from the prophets who shared what the Hebrews thought. Therefore, we can consider the poetic Psalms the *heart* book—the *this is how I'm feeling down deep in my soul* book, the *real, raw, unwoven, vulnerable truth* book. In essence, the Psalms are a glimpse into the inner life of the person sharing—a testament to the hopes, joys, doubts, dreams, sorrows, and gratitude tucked inside their human heart.

How Are You Feeling, Momma? is a collection of 31 short reflections giving you a peek into the inner life of Lisa and I as we hone in on the myriad of feelings we've grappled with as moms over the course of many years. The emotions we dive into are universal to all of us. In each chapter, you will read two perspectives on a specific emotion and corresponding Psalm scripture. One captures the emotion from my experience as a mom and the other from Lisa's vantage point.

We've been through the trenches, a combined 66 years of parenting/step-parenting/grandparenting between us. Rumor has it I'm still wandering around my house trying to find my three kids. Apparently, they left years ago because they grew up when I wasn't looking. My oldest son is 25, middle son is 23, and my daughter is 21. Although I remain in constant denial of empty nest, my hubby of 25+ years keeps gently reminding me it's time to let go. Lisa is a step-mom to a son and daughter, both in their early forties. Unlike me, Lisa accepts the changing seasons and embraces mothering from a distance with her beloved husband of 40 + years. But let's be real here; she can only do this because she has six grandbabies: five boys and one girl, ages 6-16.

The thing is, we can't avoid all the feels in mothering, but we can cry out to God for help and comfort in times of struggle. This is what Lisa and I have tried our best to do throughout our motherhood walk. We don't have all the answers because we are imperfect humans doing the 'mom thing' as best we can, like the rest of you. The words you read in this book draw from our deep wells of inexperienced experiences in hopes of bringing relief to all of us. Our honest sharing is meant to inspire you to get real about your inner life and take comfort in knowing you aren't alone in how you feel.

We hope our transparency gives you the courage to be authentic and vulnerable with others—especially God! God made us for relationship. He made us from love to *be love* in the world. In the end, the greatest benefactors of our spiritual growth are our precious offspring. Let's get inside our heart and choose to be real for their sake, if for no one else. We can do this, sisters, because God's got this.

A Note from Lisa

It's not easy for a momma to admit she's struggling. After all, motherhood is supposed to be a glorious time, and we should be reveling in its glory. Many times, we are.

But what of the other times when we feel overwhelmed and close to our wits end? That's when we're stuck in the trenches and need a lifeline. The problem? We can't walk out of the house and take a respite because we're tired and overloaded. We can't ask the kids to take care of themselves so Momma can relax with a cup of coffee and a good book.

So, what can we do that fits into the reality of Motherhood while a toddler is clinging to our knee cap and the baby screams to be fed? We can grab *How Are You Feeling, Momma?* and rest it against the toaster while we're preparing mac & cheese. We can prop up these Psalms on the napkin holder and take glances while breastfeeding. We can coax the toddler to sit on the floor with her sippy cup while baby naps so Momma can read a verse or two to sustain her.

Sometimes it takes only a few words of encouragement to nourish our souls, to keep us going. Hopefully, you'll find those few words right here.

Lean in, Momma, and know we're with you in spirit and sisterhood. And here we'll stay.

One

PSALMS FOR AFRAID MOMS

Lisa's Reflection

My son's little face was shmushed against the school bus window. Saucer-wide eyes stared back at me as I alternated waving like a crazy lady and blowing butterfly kisses. He caught one of the kisses and then began crying, just as the bus pulled away.

I continued waving until the bus turned the corner, then I dropped to my knees on the neighbor's lawn where the dam burst, releasing enough tears to water every inch. This was a milestone 'mom moment' as my first child left home to enter the grown-up world of Kindergarten.

But it could easily have been driving my car alone for the first time without me in the passenger seat directing traffic, or college drop-off when I set eyes on two sorority sisters ogling my little boy.

Capital F

Capital E

Capital A

Capital R!

I know. I know. We're supposed to give our fears over to God.

I do. We do.

However, if God mentioned this, He clearly has our number. He knows that fear and motherhood are synonyms. So how do I calm my fear and anxiety during motherhood moments that unravel me? I act like I've got everything under control—easy peasy!

I start with puffed up shoulders and some fancy swagger and accompany that air of fake confidence with the nonchalance of a worry-free woman.

It sounds as though I am lying to myself—not necessarily!

Kids call it pretending. Ever watch a 3-year-old slay a dragon? They pretend they are great warriors and PRESTO they ARE strong and capable, and the beast is buried.

Grown-ups call it "acting as if."

When we act as though we are less afraid, we can trick ourselves into believing it is true. Christopher Robin convinced Pooh that he was braver than he thought.

The Wizard of Oz gave the Cowardly Lion courage by making him believe that he had it all along.

Like a magician uses sleight of hand, I call it sleight of mind.

If you convince yourself that you can handle something, you can close your eyes and visualize it actually working.*

Well almost.

*Disclaimer: You have to practice this technique numerous times to be successful, though there's no time like the present to give it a whirl.

It's not a miracle cure. Only God can perform those feats.

However, it's a tool at our disposal that, when coupled with God's love, makes all the difference in the world.

"When anxiety was great within me, your consolation brought me joy." Psalm 94:19 (NIV)

Shelby's Reflection

Renowned psychiatrist, Elisabeth Kubler-Ross says, "There are only two primary emotions: love and fear. All positive emotions come from love, all negative emotions from fear. From love flows happiness, contentment, peace, and joy. From fear comes anger hate, anxiety, and guilt…we cannot feel these two emotions together... they're opposites. If we're in fear, we are not in a place of love. When we're in a place of love, we cannot be in a place of fear."[1]

Over the past decade, I've come to agree with her theory by noticing how love and fear operate in my life: ***love*** binds, and ***fear*** separates. Peace, joy, and contentment keep me bound to the present, grateful for my blessings. Anxiety, guilt, and worry push me out of the now and into an illusory future filled with panic and dread. The emotional power play in my mom heart took me by surprise. Although my insatiable love for my kids seemed like the driving force behind all my actions, it turns out fear can hold its own in manipulating my perspective.

In the past couple of years, my kids risked pointing out the ugly truth of my wayward parenting fears. They confided that although my intentions were formed in love, many times my intercession in their life was morbidly bereft of strength. My fearfulness was poisoning their ability to grow, accept failure, endure necessary suffering, and find their own way.

When we attempt to tackle our fears on our own by trying to control our circumstances, or in my case, pretend we are better equipped than God to manage our life, not a lot of things go right. Thinking our kids' success, security, well-being, and happiness depend on us alone is a lie. God is in control, not us. A recent fear war I had with my son brought this truth to light:

After college graduation, he accepted a gap-year fellowship opportunity to tutor math to high schoolers in inner-city Chicago—where murder rates are very high. Months before the job was to start, he was in a bar in Cleveland and just so happened to sit next to a Chicago policeman. My son asked for some advice on where to live, and the officer sternly advised him not to take the job at all—too high risk. I was sure the encounter was a blessing and a warning sign from God.

---

[1] http://www.awakin.org/read/view.php?tid=680

Um, not to my son. His response was, "Well if I die, I die. I'm not worried because I'm excited to see Jesus." He's 25. Enough said. My faith must pale in comparison.

So, I pretend prayed, i.e., worried and vexed for months, hoping my inauthentic, trustful surrender would change his mind. It was to no avail because my son forged ahead with his plans. Then, at the 11th hour, before he moved to Chicago, God showed up big with a safer opportunity. The gobs of energy I wasted on doomsday scenarios had nothing to do with it. God had a perfect plan in place all along.

Trying to do God's job when our skill-set pales in comparison will never lead to victory and often ends in hopelessness, depression, and debilitating worry—all of which prevent us from being our best for God and our children. But turning to God for comfort when we're afraid is always a move towards love. As Kubler-Ross said, "When we're in a place of love, we cannot be in a place of fear."

Turns out the Bible contains 365 verses with the phrase "fear not." God promises over and over to take care of us if we put our trust in Him. I've come to learn, through trial and error, we can take His sacred word for it.

"...in God I trust and am not afraid. What can man do to me?" Psalm 56:11 (NIV)

Personal Reflection:

What is your biggest fear as a mom, and how has God helped you push through fears in the past?

Two

PSALMS FOR ALONE MOMS

Shelby's Reflection

Perhaps one of the greatest oxymorons of all time is a 'lonely mother' when you consider the 24/7 demands of little people. But loneliness is real and hits all of us up for many reasons. Sometimes we feel alone because we've lost our identity in motherhood. Other times we're lonely because we've reached the empty nest stage. One of the worst feelings of isolation is when we pay admission to the *I'm the only one who* club. The only mom who screams at her kids, burns dinner, forgets the tooth fairy, or leaves a basement door open, resulting in a toddler plummeting down the stairs. (That'd be me. I might be the only one). Or we believe we are the only mom who fights neediness, depression, insecurity, resentment, frustration, anger. The only mom who has a child who is__________ or does __________. We run these scripts through our minds, isolating ourselves even further out of fear, shame, and remorse.

An even harder scenario is the single mom, or the mom who balances everything because her husband works seven days a week, or the Mom whose spouse is sick and needs constant medical care. All situations produce heavy and tangible loneliness.

But we're never *the only one who* anything. There are thousands of Moms out there struggling just like we are—feeling the same feelings, battling the same wars. When we dare to be authentic and vulnerable about our feelings, we'll find soul sisters ready to "me too" us into fullness and connection. I can't tell you the number of times I've gaped when finding out my experiences as a mom *aren't* unique. The ache of loneliness can evaporate in an instant when we find common ground with another.

Admitting our sense of isolation is no easy task. In fact, doing so can feel humiliating. This is where God comes in. If we cry out to Him first by saying, *"Look at me and help me! I'm all alone and in big trouble."* (Psalm 25:16 MSG), we might find out God has the perfect friend or even a total stranger ready to meet us where we're at. He works wonders that way. All we need to do is be on the lookout.

Lisa's Reflection

Being a mom can sometimes be a lonely experience despite the beauty and glory of this role.

It seems contradictory to logic that we can feel alone amidst our children and all the daily routines that consume us, mind, body, and soul.

Yet have we not all found ourselves sitting in the middle of the living room rug on the verge of tears or well past the floodgates bursting open and wondering *why*? What's wrong with me? I have everything! I should be grateful for these miracles.

We keep these feelings to ourselves for fear that we will be judged. We hold on to the shame and guilt and never realize that the mom next door is sitting on HER living room rug contemplating the same feelings.

The vastness of our responsibility as moms could break us if we gave it too much thought.

So when we feel alone there are ways to combat the aloneness and ones I am certain are God-approved:

- Take a walk outside with your little ones, and smile at a stranger; it humanizes everything and causes an immediate change in perspective. You might well bump into another lonely mom, and if you help her feel better, it helps you as well!
- Sing! God gave us a voice so we could rejoice, and there's no better way to lift your spirit than to burst

out in song. Grab your childhood microphone (hairbrush) and let it rip! If the neighbor chooses to close her window to drown you out, even better.

- Look through a photo album, which is a scrapbook of your life and a glorious reminder of the miles you have walked to get here. It, too, brings perspective back into focus.
- Take a look in the mirror and say 'Thank You' to YOU for doing an extraordinary job under incredibly difficult and challenging circumstances every day. Isn't motherhood beautiful and so challenging simultaneously?

When you find yourself stuck in the muck of motherhood, in the trenches where we all have been, open your Bible and read Psalm 40:2 (NIV): *"He lifted me out of the slimy pit, out of the mud and mire; he set my feet on a rock and gave me a firm place to stand."*

Personal Reflection:

What is one action you can take today to feel connected?

Three

PSALMS FOR BURNED-OUT MOMS

Lisa's Reflection

This motherhood gig is exhausting.

Not the type of exhausting that comes from running a race or hiking a mountain.

This is the 'feels like you went 10 rounds with Joe Frazier,' except on an emotional, psychological, and spiritual level, not only a physical one. Surely anyone that has read the mom job description would have a hard time believing it requires the efforts of just one worker as opposed to 20.

So, when it reaches the point where you do not feel you have what it takes to go one minute more without breaking, how do you find the strength to go one minute more without breaking?

Imagine if 'Mom Burnout' was a legitimate diagnosis that permitted doctors to write prescriptions recommending long naps and staycations, home-delivered meals and massages for the tired aching bones!

Let's get past delusional and down to reality.

You're burned out. You're entitled. But you notice that no empathy cards are arriving daily in your mailbox. Every momma you know has visited this same trench.

Some wade in deeper than others on certain days, but all of us have experienced the muck of motherhood and felt burnt to a crisp. You're at the brink. You're about to lose it and *kaboom*!

Hello, God!

Really? Hello, God?

Yep! Hello, God!

And not a moment too soon! Motherhood does not afford us the luxury to stop what we're doing on a whim to regenerate, rejuvenate, and re-energize. We have to be able to chat with God while one baby hangs in a sling on our front, one toddler has hold of our left shin, one is battling to climb our right leg, and one is calling from naptime that her fish mobile stopped.

What's cool about talking with God is He hears us above the noise and chaos and in short, staccato sentences without commas or periods.

He gets the gist of our burnout status without us having to explain ourselves.

All we basically need to say is, "Hey, God, excuse me, but I have nothing left here."

Telling Him releases something from us. It gives us one extra breath or two. Sometimes that's all it takes to get us through— that and a few bites of chocolate with a sip of wine.

"Because you are my help, I sing in the shadow of your wings." Psalm 63:7 (NIV)

Shelby's Reflection

Mom burnout happens for countless reasons because, family life. Maybe God's to blame since He built moms with full-throttle, multi-tasking capabilities. When we need to get a million things done, we get a million and a half things done without even thinking. Problem is, it's a horrible superpower because instead of calling on God to revitalize our spent spirit, we often let exhaustion spill over into the mix of everyday living, making us sick or super cranky or despondently delirious. Then all our family members need to beware because #Momisaraginglunatic.

Jesus said in His famous Sermon on the Mount, *"You are blessed when you are at the end of your rope. With less of you, there is more of God and his rule."* Matthew 5:3 (MSG) Just last week I said in my famous rant to the universe, "Really, God? I'll get more of you and your rule when I'm burned out at the end of my rope? I'm a frayed knot." Pretty sure I heard the Creator of the universe chuckle. Hmf.

As a survivor of 25 years of end of rope scenarios from raising three children all born within 42 months, I guess my cup does runneth over with the "blessings" of the first Beatitude. I was blessed when working from home and flying solo in taking care of my three littles while hubby worked out of town all week. Even more blessed when all three kids were in sports, in different leagues, with different game times. Apparently blessed beyond when trying to build a consulting business, serve at church, and manage three teens whose lives and emotions were sprouting in all different directions. At the time, you could have fooled me.

The struggle is real in trying to find more of God and His rule while crossing off an endless to-do list. How in the world do we fit in one more thing? The only solution I found was this: the more we stay *present,* the more 'clock time' is available. So, when we ruminate over yesterday or fret over tomorrow (or even the next hour), we consume time in dispensing mental energy, like depleting RAM on a computer. But when we are present in the *now,* focusing only on what's in front of us, we bend time in our favor because our mind is free of past regrets (yelled at the kids) and future worries (I'll never get all this done). The extra sand in the hourglass creates time for us to commune with God. Even a quick prayer can be enough to recharge us. Heck, even a simple, "Jesus, help me," can make all the difference in the world.

"You've always given me breathing room, a place to get away from it all, a lifetime pass to your safe-house, an open invitation as your guest." Psalm 61:3-4 (MSG)

Personal Reflection:

Is there something in your life you can eliminate right now to create some breathing space?

Four

PSALMS FOR CHEATED MOMS

Shelby's Reflection

Oh, the ways a mom can feel cheated. We give and give, often with little appreciation in return. The situations capable of brewing up a sense of missing out, feeling let down, or being treated unfairly are limitless; some minor and others gut-wrenching or long-suffering. While it's true we empty ourselves into our children by insatiable instinct and desire, even the Mother Theresas of the world can furrow a brow over feeling taken for granted.

As a SAHM living two miles from the schools, my kids considered me on call 24/7. At a moment's notice, I was asked to drop off forgotten assignments, bring lunch money, or whip up an appetizer for an afternoon class party. Never mind I worked from home as a self-employed consultant with real clients I needed to serve. In my kids' eyes, running out 'real quick' and doing something for them was no big deal. More times than not, I agreed to meet their needs, only to stew in silence over their expectations and my inability to say no.

I'd convinced myself being a SAHM obligated me to answer their beck and call—a privilege to be grateful for. But then I felt cheated because my kids undervalued my job and other responsibilities besides being a mom. The truth is, I set myself up to feel slighted. Not prioritizing my schedule, shielding my kids from the consequences of irresponsibility, and staying silent on my feeling used festered resentment. Then I'd lose my marbles over something minor, leaving my kids wide-eyed and confused. I'd hear them whispering things like, "What's wrong with Mom?" followed by, "NO idea. She flipped out because I left my dishes in the sink?!"

Here's the thing. Kids' frontal lobes—the reasoning section—don't develop in full until 25ish. Come to think of it, perhaps my front brain hasn't reached full 'think it through' status at 48. Anyway, kids are almost incapable on their own of thinking beyond their somewhat selfish requests or ingratitude, let alone surmise 'Mom must feel like we're taking her for granted.' Over time, I learned to be honest with my kids, instead, sharing with them all I was doing on their behalf and asked them to be mindful and pick up their own slack. Believe it or not, they got my perspective and even apologized with, "Why didn't you just say something sooner?" Kids and their wise counsel.

Although I felt cheated, disconnect was the real problem. If we want our family to be on the same page, we are best to communicate our feelings, create healthy boundaries, and set realistic expectations. This is what the Hebrews were doing in the book of Psalms: letting God know how they felt so they could connect heart-to-heart. What if we commit to sharing our feelings with God and our kids on a regular basis? Chances are, clearing the air will allow new appreciation to birth, which creates space for love to expand.

"I cry out to the LORD; I plead for the LORD's mercy, I pour out my complaints before him and tell him of my troubles." Psalm 142:1-2 (NLT)

Lisa's Reflection

"When I grow up I am going to be president of a company and give all my friends a job so they can buy hamsters and ferrets and give their parents an allowance."

That's the journal entry of a seven-year-old girl. Fast-forward 39 years. The offer to become president of a corporation arrived on the Wednesday before Thanksgiving.

I held the joyous announcement and decided to share it with the entire family during our traditional holiday dinner. During appetizers, my beautiful stepdaughter Jennifer, now 8 months pregnant with our first grandchild, told us she also had an announcement to share with the family.

I let her go first.

"We've decided that I will go back to work after the baby is born, and we'd like you to be our full-time nanny."

I had been looking down at my plate trying to dip my mushrooms into as much sautéed butter as possible, so when I looked up, it was with curiosity as to who the 'you' was that Jennifer was referring to.

Nineteen pairs of eyes were looking at me.

I never shared my exciting announcement and played it down to be something so insignificant it could wait until dessert. Dessert came and went, and so did we.

Four days later I met with the Chairman of the Board and resigned from my position before it began. The Chairman was dumbfounded. No more so than I.

In less than four weeks, I was frantically searching for my beautiful grandson's binky lodged under a couch cushion and feeling cheated out of my one chance in a lifetime to head up a corporation.

Instead of jetting to meetings across the globe, I was changing poopy diapers. Instead of writing notes for my staff, I was writing down amounts of formula taken every two hours.

One morning in-between a colicky episode and a burp, my grandson grabbed my thumb and smiled up at me. In that one precise second, he became the center of my universe.

It's an on-going love affair that rivals even Christopher Robin and Pooh.

Hammocks (where we lay down to count clouds) and tree houses (where we hold court with dinosaurs and dragons) are our best-kept secret places.

We let ladybugs crawl on our knees and coax butterflies into soft landings in our palms.

We've danced in rainstorms and watched our fair share of toy boats in the toilet making tidal waves.

When no one is looking, we lick gummy bears and stick them to the front porch. The UPS man thinks we have a masterpiece in our midst.

And to think I once felt cheated out of being president of a company. Instead, God chose THIS once-in-a-lifetime role for me.

"Cheated" is no longer a word in my vocabulary.

"Abundantly blessed" is.

"Because of my integrity you uphold me and set me in your presence forever." Psalm 41:12 (NIV)

Personal Reflection:

In what way are you feeling cheated right now? Ask God for a solution.

Five

PSALMS FOR CONFUSED MOMS

Lisa's Reflection

I remember growing up hearing the phrase "dazed and confused" and wondered if it referred to me after an algebra exam. Then I became a grown-up (at least in number form), and the phrase took on a whole new meaning.

I am convinced that God coined this phrase to explain a mom's reaction each time her child enters a new phase of development.

When we as moms finally come close to mastering their mood swings and behaviors, desires and words, then—*poof*—that phase disappears and is replaced with a new and more interesting (notice my choice of word) one that is more baffling and confusing than the last.

How come there is no rollover effect?

In school you take pre-requisites. You cannot enroll in intermediate French without successfully studying and passing beginner's French. Then your knowledge is expected to rollover. It's cumulative.

So how come, when it comes to childrearing, what you think you learned when they were two does not apply at three? That is why I have always been a firm proponent of a University for Mothers, to be staffed by the warriors who came before us.

These learned women could instruct us in the fundamentals of motherhood, from birth through empty nest, and help address our confusion. We could even enroll online and listen with the one babe in our arms, the toddler straddling our leg, and the newborn in the bassinet.

Who better equipped to help us navigate our confusion than those who went before and survived? Wouldn't we all feel so much better if we had a reliable and trustworthy source to discuss our daily motherhood dilemmas with?

Everyone says that's what Mom friends are for, and though I wholeheartedly agree, sometimes you need an unbiased stranger with no investment in protecting your feelings to give it to you straight.

I, for one, would be more than grateful to have a fellow mom, who already waded through all the muck, to be my helper in negotiating what lies ahead. Then again, perhaps I would like to remain naïve and innocent and believe that everything I already learned by raising a three-year-old will apply to the newly minted four-year-old.

If that's not possible, then I will continue what I do best.

That is, check in with God daily or more at the times when my mom confusion catapults me into crazy, and I respond by desperately searching for kisses (of the chocolate variety)!

"*You guide me with your counsel, and afterward you will take me into glory.*" Psalm 73:24 (NIV)

Shelby's Reflection

Not sure about you, but there's a good chance I can count on two fingers the number of times I've felt 100% certain about what I was doing as a mom. Lack of understanding in every age and stage, coupled with bewilderment during crises big and small is more the norm. We sashay into this gig with very little clarity from day one, and just when we think we've mastered a particular aspect of raising kiddos, something else stumps us: How should I respond to this? What actions will I take to curb that? Where do I go for help? When should I intervene? Why do my kids think, say, and do all these things? Will I ever get my act together?

Because of the chaos going on in today's world, our uncertainty about all things "life" compounds our confusion about all things motherhood. We have no idea what tomorrow will bring, or the next five minutes. God created us to live and enjoy His creation—the awe, wonder, beauty, and mind-blowing uniqueness of everything He's crafted. But He also warned us of the tribulation, strife, and disaster we are destined to experience.

The dissonance creates all kinds of confusion on how to best raise up, protect, and ensure the well-being of our children. All the uncertainty takes a toll on our mom hearts. We want nothing more than to do our best for our kids, and we ache for them to experience more goodness than wickedness. So what do we do to find peace and clarity?

As enticing as it sounds, we can't keep our kids in a bubble. Life marches on in any direction humanity chooses to push, and if we're alive, we're destined to be a part of the cadence. So the only solution I have is this: point both ourselves and our kids to Jesus—who is Love. Love knows the answers to our questions. Love knows the way, paves the way, is the way to certainty. Let's challenge ourselves and write the following Psalm on our doors and put a sticky note in our car as a reminder to entrust all the comings and goings of our days to Love.

"Show me the right path, O Lord; point out the road for me to follow. Lead me by your truth and teach me, for you are the God who saves me. All day long I put my hope in you." Psalm 25:4-5 (NLT)

Personal Reflection:

Who might God use to help you navigate through your present confusion?

Six

PSALMS FOR DEPRESSED MOMS

Shelby's Reflection

The topic of depression is near and not so dear to me. When praying about how to speak on this very real struggle, God nudged me to dig out my old journals. I knew exactly what He wanted me to find and thought about arguing for half a second. But I knew better. For everything, there is a time and season. These reflections are about honest emotions, so I'd be doing a disservice in holding back something I can share for His glory and potentially your benefit.

I opened my 2005 journal and found the raw script God wanted me to share. The backdrop of this dark night of my soul was me alone, sprawled out on the carpet—face down, raging at the machine of life, straining to hear anything from God's still small voice amid the sobs and emptiness inside me. Although He didn't respond, I kept wailing until this personal psalm of lament found its way onto the page:

TRIALS
They suck me into the abyss
And fill my spirit with rage
I am lost, I am angry
I am completely empty

Lord, why can't I love you
The way you ask me to?
Why must I allow doubt—Satan's nasty uppercut

To knock me out every time we step in the ring?

When will I stand firm on two feet
With a heart of gold and spirit of joy
That can never be shaken?

Why must I always turn away from You
When darkness falls upon me?
Why, Lord?

You give me chance after chance to see the Light
To hold on to Your promises
And turn to Glory
Instead of filth and death.

But my soul is ravaged
By the grip of disappointment, failure,
Missed opportunity.

I am sinking AGAIN into quicksand
And I need Your hand to pull me out.

PULL ME OUT, LORD.
Please

The next morning, I dragged myself to morning Mass, battered and bruised from the inside out. The first person to greet me was our deacon, a long-time family friend.

"How are you, sweetie?"

I crumbled into his arms and wept—not an ounce of strength left in me to pretend. Although I don't recall speaking any words, the Spirit of the Lord in me must have groaned,

> *"Me? I'm a mess. I'm nothing and have nothing:*
> *make something of me.*
> *You can do it; you've got what it takes—*
> *but God, don't put it off."* (Psalm 40:17 MSG)

Shortly after, my deacon pressed a business card into my hand.

"This is my friend, also a deacon, and a licensed therapist for 30+ years. Go see him."

The abridged version is I went to the therapist… still do. Years of re-writing a broken script in my mind and proper medication for what would result in a bipolar diagnosis are why I'm able to write this story today. God met me where I was on that somber night and then sent a helper to greet me the next morning. Even though my journal is still difficult to read 13 years later, God continues to pull favor from the dust of my ashes. I'm living proof that God desires to heal, deliver, redeem, restore, renew, and love us forward.

So cry out, mommas. God gave humans the wisdom to counsel, scientists the smarts to create healing elements, and angels on earth the ability to console and guide us. Accept these gifts. Be well. You have my heart.

Lisa's Reflection

What happens when the mom of a beautiful newborn does not feel the unbridled joy and bliss she expected to experience?

What happens when that new mom is privately thinking thoughts about her newborn that are so unbearable to process that even she cannot face herself in the mirror?

There's guilt.

There's shame.

Sometimes self-loathing.

Always heartache.

Who does she turn to?

A powerful stigma faces this mom, and she may not feel comfortable sharing with anyone, not even the closest of loved ones.

She is alone.

She feels helpless.

Hopelessness lurks around the corner.

How does she bring herself to face each day with lingering anguish and a soul that feels empty inside?

She doesn't unless we as women warriors recognize the symptoms of DEPRESSION and step up to the plate, welcoming her in with open arms.

That's the hard part.

Moms are pretty awesome at hiding their feelings.

There's an answer:

- If we as women make it easier for a mom to be genuine and honest about what she is facing without fear of reprisal;
- If we make it acceptable to say, "I'm not okay, and I'm not enjoying being a Mom";
- If we reassure a Mom that we're here for the duration and we're not judging.

Those are the beginning steps.

Then we encourage this courageous mom to seek a professional who will provide therapy and perhaps medication if deemed necessary.

There's another stigma right there.

A mom needing medication to cope with motherhood?

No, a mom relying on medication to cope with depression.

Next, we ask God to stop by and stay awhile so He can give this mom some comfort and peace of mind that she is not going to battle alone.

It's a three-way street.

Women Warriors + Professional Counseling + God = A mom being rescued from the darkness and once again able to find her joy.

P.S. Another beautiful baby snuggles in the arms of a contented mom who smiles from the inside out, radiating gratitude and love.

"*Hear my voice when I call LORD; be merciful to me and answer me*." Psalm 27:7 (NIV)

Personal Reflection:
What's holding you back from asking for help?

Seven

PSALMS FOR DISTRESSED MOMS

Lisa's Reflection

I use the word distressed in a sentence, and my kids think I'm talking about jeans. My husband thinks I'm talking about the wood on the coffee table. Wrong on both counts! I'm talking about my daily dose of self-induced anxiety caused by motherhood's little concerns:

- What happens if the diorama I made with my daughter is not an accurate enough depiction of Native American life in the 1800's? Will she get an 'F' and flunk out of school?
- Could the lettuce I bought be contaminated with pesticides? Worse yet, Listeria?
- If I invite 15 classmates to my child's party and only two show, how will I not collapse from the heartache of watching my child handle the devastation of being rejected?
- Is it possible that a babysitter does not know the peanut allergy rule, so she packs a brownie with nuts for the kid who sits next to my son's desk?
- The weather forecast calls for thunderstorms for the Cub Scouts' first outing. Do I send him or feign illness to protect him from being struck by lightning?

- I think my daughter's gums look swollen from eating the backyard dirt. Could it be trench mouth?
- Why isn't my mother-in-law enforcing homework rules while I'm at work? Should I try and get my husband to intervene and risk losing my most reliable sitter?
- How can I send my daughter to a pasta party at a teammate's house without meeting the parents? They could be deranged. Who knows nowadays?
- If that coach sidelines my kid one more time, who is going to hold me down on the bleachers and assist me in stifling my disappointment?
- How do I explain to the pediatrician that my child only eats mini-pancakes at every meal, without sounding like a dismal failure?
- How do I explain to my child that he can't eat just mini-pancakes at every meal, without witnessing a seismic meltdown?
- How do I explain to my husband that our son, despite every effort of mine to introduce new and healthy food choices, won't eat anything but mini-pancakes at every meal, without seeing his arched eyebrow and 'hearing' his unspoken admonishment that if HE were in charge of mealtimes our son would be dining on all sorts of foods?
- How do I explain to my mother-in-law that her grandson will not eat her ziti, without witnessing HER arched eyebrow and the silent daggers?

This is only two hours' worth of distress. I'm merely getting started. Stop by after dinner. Us moms are on a roll by then!

"Look on my affliction and my distress and take away all my sins." Psalm 25:18 (NIV)

Shelby's Reflection

When our second son was five days old, he stopped breathing. By the time the ambulance arrived, he was coughing and crying, air filling up his lungs once again. But we still had to transport him to the hospital for tests: EKG, spinal tap, blood panel, etc. I was the ripe age of 25 when a firestorm of unknowns blazed at me from every direction.

My infant daughter rolled nine feet on her first try (who knew?), into the landing space of our second floor and then tumbled down all but the last step before I caught her. After a shameful trip to the ER, she was fine.

Our oldest son endured hurtful bullying for five years, grades 4-8, to the point I convinced the administration to let me implement an anti-bullying program. The effects of the bullying were far-reaching. My mom blood simmered for years as I worried and vexed about his damaged self-esteem.

These are only a handful of the times my mom heart has been rung out hard and hung up wet. Trying to describe the inner roar of a mom's soul when her child's health and well-being is at risk is pointless. I guess distressed will have to do.

As life would have it, those moments were only a precursor to what would be the most horrifying and distressing experience I've had to date as a mom. Our town's high school was the target of a merciless school shooting in 2012. My kids were senior, sophomore, and freshman at the time. By God's grace, they're still with me. I can't say the same blessing fell upon every mother because three young boys lost their lives, one remains paralyzed, and another was wounded. The emotional scarring on the entire school, all of us as families, and the extended community is impossible to quantify. But despite the wreckage, God was and still is with us and for us.

So, mommas, what do we do when we find ourselves in a moment or season of distress? We cry out to God with all our might. Look for Him everywhere. Scream, yell, beg, curse up at the heavens if need be. Trust me, I did during the shooting experience.

God can handle the real and raw. He knows our heart, so no use veiling our anguish. King David never held back his sorrow and torment. Neither should we. God loves us. He's going to get us through NO MATTER WHAT. He only asks us to believe and hold on. When we can't, we hold on for each other. Together.

"But in my distress I cried out to the Lord; yes, I prayed to my God for help. He heard me from his sanctuary; my cry to him reached his ears." – King David Psalm 18:6 (NLT)

Personal Reflection:

Do you trust God is always with you in your distress? Why or why not?

Eight

PSALMS FOR ELATED MOMS

(Lisa, Shelby, and God pretend-met at Starbucks the other day. Here is a transcript of their satirical chitchat about elation.)

Shelby: God, I can't thank you enough for meeting with us this a.m. I mean, I guess you meet with us every day. Like all day. As in, you are literally with us and in us. Haha! But the "in person" thing? No words.

Lisa: God, forgive me for sounding ungrateful, but you couldn't have chosen Dunkin' Donuts? I still have $2.86 left on my card! Had I known that somewhere along the way it would mean a face-to-face with you, Lord, I would have at least written you a poem and made you a cherry pie, put on my Sunday best, and taken my heart medication before I left the house because in your presence an arrhythmia is surely on the horizon. Wait, you can fix that, so I'm okay! Thank God!

God: (chuckles) You are welcome, my daughters. What really warms my heart is how you two of differing faiths and so-called contrasting opinions on life matters have come together to talk with Yours Truly. The willingness to accept one another beyond any opposing views is what true love is; it's what I Am, and what you are—love.

A little secret between you and me — you ladies have much more in common than you think. I made you both in my image. I don't change. Only humanity's perception of me gets skewed, the whole free will thing, which I know causes you suffering. But the endgame is so worth it when you come to realize how beautiful life is and you choose to follow me and to love others the way I do.

Shelby: Can I go on record and say you are one amazing Creator? Just wow. As for this beautiful woman next to me, she's so easy to love. Thank you for blowing the winds of serendipity so we would meet. She's the real deal. Well, of course, you already know that. Duh.

Lisa: You know, when I used to conjure you up in my mind, you always looked like a cross between Jesus and Moses. (God grins). This is the happiest I have ever been in my life. God, did you ever hear of happy dancing? That's what my soul is doing right this very moment! Shelby encouraged me to join her on this journey because of her abundant and glorious love for you. She knew because you knew that I would willingly oblige. It has become one of the treasured honors of my life!

God: Ah yes, the happy dance. I'm especially fond of when my children embrace their inner exuberance and contentment. Regarding your book journey, I love when humans hear my whispers.

Lisa: Can I ask you something, God? Remember that scene in *The Ten Commandments* when Moses gets mad at you because he thinks you have forsaken him? Was that an accurate portrayal, or did Cecil B. DeMille take poetic license with your history?

God: To each his own.

Shelby: What about the scene in *History of the World* with Mel Brooks when Moses carries three stone tablets down the mountain proclaiming, "O hear me, all take heed. The LORD, the LORD Jehovah, has given unto you these 15 (one tablet drops and shatters on the ground), 10…10 Commandments for all to obey." What were those five other laws anyway? And how come Moses' proclamation fail didn't make a mark in your Holy Book?

God: Have you ever read this message in a fortune cookie: "Don't believe everything you hear and only half of what you see"? Well, consider these words' sage advice. Beyond that, do your best to listen to me, and I will answer all you need to know when you need to know it. Always guard your hearts and stay focused on love. I have to say, the commandment scene in *History of the World* did crack me up. Still SMH. Clever.

Shelby: God, the way you have been answering my mom prayers and working in my kids' lives lately is nothing short of miraculous. I wanted to take this opportunity to tell you how elated and grateful I am for your blessings. Sometimes I forget to say thanks, which is rude, all things mercy, grace, healing, guidance, unconditional love considered. So here goes my litany of praise (emphasis mine):

"I will give thanks to you, LORD, with all my heart; I will tell of all your wonderful deeds.[2] *The LORD is my strength and my shield; my heart trusts in him, he helps me (with all my needs).*[3] *Let us come before him with thanksgiving and extol him with music and song.*[4] *Praise the LORD. Give thanks to the LORD, for he is good; his love endures (all day long)."*[5]

(God's eyes soften, taking on the gaze of a loving father)

Lisa: God, you're awfully quiet.

God: My child, I am always listening.

Lisa: Do you know that sometimes I doubt that you hear me?

God: (giggles) I do know.

Lisa: I once said something really mean about you that I thought you needed hearing aids.

God: I heard that one! My angels got a kick out of your comment! The truth is, sometimes I wish I could turn the volume down.

(A beeper sounds. God's beeper.)

Lisa: Please don't leave! I haven't had a chance to tell you all the things I'm elated over! I want to, *"Sing to the Lord a new song; sing to the Lord, all the earth!"* Psalm 96:1 (NIV)

---

2 Psalm 9:1 (NIV)

3 Psalm 28:7 (NIV)

4 Psalm 95:2-3 (NIV)

5 Psalm 106:1 (NIV)

God: You don't have to. I already know by watching your joy. Thank you for honoring me by cherishing and using the gifts I have given you. Your elation is my joy and reminds me I'm doing a good job! And like any mom will tell you, we all could use a little pat on the back every so often. Even me!

Shelby: Well this has been an a-ma-za-zing experience, God. Thanks for taking time out of your hectic cosmic schedule to meet with us. I do have one more important question for you to answer. Did you pre-plan the Indians vs. Yankees playoff series? What were the odds of our two cities' teams competing against each other during our journey of writing about these mom emotions? I mean, we can handle the whole Jewish/Christian contrast, but a baseball rivalry? A bit much don't you think?

God: Some things are better off left a mystery, dear child. My best advice is to play nice like you do with the rest of your worldviews and enjoy the moment. I appreciate your gratitude for my meeting with you, but no thanks necessary. I'm especially fond of sipping the fruits of the coffee beans I created and breaking banana nut bread with friends. But if I'm honest, the price of this coffee is a bit over the multiverse. Yet, for some reason, you humans continue to herd in and out of these places. But I get it. The whole free will thing. Sure can cost you a pretty penny! LOL That pumpkin spice though. Genius.

Personal Reflection:

Write about how your mom heart feels during moments of elation, and describe what situations evoke such a warm emotion.

Nine

PSALMS FOR GUILTY MOMS

Shelby's Reflection

Mom guilt.

It's the worst.

And since we expect ourselves to be perfecto, the screw-ups tend to linger in our hearts like a strong red onion in our mouth. No matter how many times we brush, we just can't get rid of the taste. It takes a bit of time. Likewise, no matter how many times we ask God to forgive our mom fails, we just can't seem to curb the gnawing feeling of shame. It takes a bit of time.

Mom guilt takes on many forms: not spending enough time with the kids, saying something regrettable, not saying something you should have, forgetting something important, wishing you could be alone for 10 minutes or a month and acting like a crab apple when you can't.

How many of you deal with guilt over the types of meals you prepare, activities you fail to plan, limits you don't enforce? What about when you miss attending a very important game, event, or milestone because of work or other scheduling conflicts? How about the heart wrench of deciding whether to go to junior's soccer game or daughter's recital?

The guilt is awful.

The self-bashing is even worse.

Feeling guilty can often be the correct emotional response, except when it isn't. So why, for the love of mercy, do we keep ourselves on the hook of shame? We know we can jump off any time. God reminds us over and over His mercy endures forever, His forgiveness drawing from a perpetual well of grace.

Do you think we eat shame like it's life-giving manna because of self-love? As in, a serious lack thereof? If our emotional baseline is *I don't like who I see in the mirror,* then we're doomed when we think we've failed, and even worse, when we make real mistakes. Anything affirming a false reality of self adds another layer to the onion of remorse.

Moms, we need to stop hating on ourselves in general. When we screw up, God says to apologize, repent, and allow the waters of mercy to cleanse us into new beginnings. The end.

"Yes, what joy for those
whose record the Lord has cleared of guilt,
whose lives are lived in complete honesty!
Finally, I confessed all my sins to you
and stopped trying to hide my guilt.
I said to myself, "I will confess my rebellion to the Lord."
And you forgave me! All my guilt is gone." Psalm 32:2, 4-5 (NLT)

And it's not just God who offers loving forgiveness. Our kids are super quick to accept an apology, no grudges attached. But we need self-love to believe God's plan to its fruition, "...and you forgave me! All my guilt is gone."

Growing in this type of love sometimes means a white-knuckled assault against self-preservation. We need a high emotional pain tolerance to risk removing the veils hiding who we think we are so we can love who we really are, as seen through the eyes of God. How we love ourselves impacts how we love our children. Oh, how we long to love them well. God help us to start loving ourselves well first, which begins and ends with genuinely knowing and loving you.

Lisa's Reflection

The time you asked me to read "that big book with the blue elephant" for the 35th time and I said, "NO," in a booming voice, and you shrunk away from me and into your blanket fort.

The time you asked me to help you fix your blanket fort so we could both stay snuggly and I said, "It's nap time. Maybe later."

The time I privately wished for a hot steaming cup of coffee instead of sharing your chocolate milk with the gummy bears swirling around.

The time I threw out one of the thousand Miss Kitty drawings and then lied and said I gave it to Grandma.

How about when I had my mini temper tantrum after you dropped all the Lucky Charm marshmallows into the toilet bowl to see if they would sink or swim?

Let's not forget me doing my best imitation of the Hulk when you missed the bus for the third time in one week, and I blamed you for not getting up in time when I was your alarm clock, and I was the one who overslept.

I cringe at this one: You put two plastic pails and shovels in the sandbox so we could play together and dig to China, and I did not feel like getting dirty. Those little pails and their partners are indelibly printed in my mind—etched in my soul, an opportunity missed.

I could go on forever it seems, listing out those moments where you came in second or third or not at all when looking for your favorite playmate to share space with you. And now I want to play, and you're too grown up to consider the requests. I am wallowing in guilt. I want EVERY moment back.

But I think that this guilt chews my soul from the inside and forces me to miss out on the possibility of new moments right in front of me. I know. I'm human. But 'Jewish mom' guilt is powerful enough to scoop you up and deposit you in another state.

Yet if God forgives me, why not work on forgiving myself?

Tell you what, my beautiful son; may I make a bargain with you?

I will release my guilt if you promise not to remind me of any other times that I might use to wallow further.

Hey, I actually am feeling slightly lighter!

This might work!

Let me grab that steaming cup of hot coffee and take a sip.

"I confess my iniquity: I am troubled by my sin." Psalm 38:18 (NIV)

Personal Reflection:

If you struggle with guilt, compare how you deal with the emotion versus how you want your child to handle guilt. Is there a difference?

Ten

PSALMS FOR HATEFUL MOMS

Lisa's Reflection

Did you know that a mom who breastfeeds is doing right by her baby, and one who uses formula should be crucified?

I bet you didn't know that a SAHM is far more loving and caring than her 'working outside of the home' counterpart.

Have you read articles about one of the biggest criminals of all?

No?

Let me enlighten you!

It's the mom who places her child in daycare! Have you met one of THOSE yet?

I forgot one: the mom who insists on ignoring her child who is in the throes of a full-fledged temper tantrum, thus disturbing the shopping experiences of some more knowledgeable moms.

Yep, HER!

Lest we not overlook another inferior mom, how about the one who allows her child to eat pancakes for every meal? There should be penalties for that one!

Wait, did you hear about the mom who refuses to use "timeouts" in her home? She really could use a talk with a child psychologist.

See where I am going with all of this?

Do you know who perpetuates these HATEFUL and disturbing stereotypes, giving rise and credence to them every day?

MOMS!

The very women we all need to rely on in our sisterhood to rally around us with encouragement and support, love and compassion.

Seriously! STOP JUDGING!

The hateful words and condescending attitudes are affecting so many mothers who are trying their very best in often more challenging and difficult situations than we could possibly understand. Some are holding on by a mere thread, and the hateful attacks on their parenting style are pushing them to the edge.

We weaken all moms when we stand in judgment.

Unless we can say that God personally shared with us that OUR way is the one and only RIGHT way, we must back up and show some decency.

One day, our "perfect approach" may fall short, and when we call upon another mom for her advice and a shoulder to lean on, we may find ourselves left in the dust.

Let's start acting toward one another like the loving women God put on this earth.

If not, we risk a chasm between us that will harm generations to come, and we will only have ourselves to blame!

"For the Lord is righteous, he loves justice; the upright will see his face." Psalm 11:7(NIV)

Shelby's Reflection

"Hate. Hate. Hate. Double hate. Loooaaattthhhh entirely," said the Grinch about certain Whos in Whoville.

And, if I'm honest, also says Shelby about certain things in Thingville, causing me fear and anxiety over my children's future.

Are we called not to hate? I don't know. Hate has a genuine ring sometimes. I even heard a priest use the sentiment in a sermon last week; "I hated my second-grade teacher," his exact words. At least he's honest.

Because shouldn't we hate some stuff? Like evil for example? Evil is the seed of so many vile offshoots in our world: violence, porn, trafficking, abuse. All realities choking out a peaceful existence for our children.

So, yes, I hate these things and every other trace of DNA linked to the great deceiver. Satan preys on our kids like a cowardly lion—enticing them with promises of inclusion, acceptance, happiness, and love if only they take a bite from the apple of alcohol, drugs, sex, power, control. What about the guarantee of prestige through mental thumb wars battled on cell phones? Evil taunts our kids to believe whatever they bully down must cause them to go up in significance.

Then there's politics. Oh, do I despise this realm. I've made a mental pact never to discuss politics in my writing, which I won't. I make mention only to share how my disdain caused me to be a lousy role model of a mom last election cycle. The rhetoric was like hate on steroids. The insults, brashness, arrogance, lies, and contradictions et al. disgusted me. Then I said not nice things, thankfully only to a handful of people who know my true heart.

The thing is, God does hate some stuff. According to Solomon, *"There are six things the LORD hates—no, seven things he detests: haughty eyes, a lying tongue, hands that kill the innocent, a heart that plots evil, feet that race to do wrong, a false witness who pours out lies, a person who sows discord in a family."* Proverbs 6:16-19 (NIV) Goodness gracious, do we see these behaviors in today's world.

As for me, what I really hated during the election was my behavior. My actions were, well, hateful. I allowed the vitriol to overcome me, to separate me from the ultimate victor in any race—God. Satan got between me and my everything. I became the very thing God hates, the words spilling out of my mouth sowing discord among brethren.

So, I stopped. Cold turkey. Done. Enough. No more news or Twitter. No more trying to figure anything out. Instead, I fell to my knees where I should have been all along—surrendered, humble, silent. Prayerful. Because God says the only weapon against evil and hate is love. Nothing else works. God is love. Since we are made in God's image, love is also who we are, what we're made of, and why we're here. So I think the only way to overcome the hate and evil is through full surrender to healing love. Hate feels good in the moment because its thick claws sinking into our angry skin gives a weird relief. But love feels better. Softer. All encompassing. Less messy.

Love washes over our kiddos. Hate stains. Oh, LORD, help us to love. Help us to choose you.

"Be still in the presence of the Lord, and wait patiently for him to act. Don't worry about evil people who prosper or fret about their wicked schemes. Stop being angry! Turn from your rage! Do not lose your temper—it only leads to harm. For the wicked will be destroyed, but those who trust in the Lord will possess the land." Psalm 37:7-9 (NLT)

Personal Reflection:

Is there someone or some situation stealing your joy, and how can you release the vitriol?

Eleven

PSALMS FOR IMPATIENT MOMS

Shelby's Reflection

"Hurry up, let's go! What are you doing? You said you'd be ready to leave 10 minutes ago; 'just need to brush my teeth' was your promise. Why does this happen every. single. Sunday? Ugh!"

Such was my prayerful preparation and mindful meditation before screeching out the door to church when my kids were all home. Nothing like getting my heart ready to worship the Lord! The problem is, the worshiping part never started until halfway through the service, because I spent the first quarter talking myself off a pew and the second begging God for mercy over my impatient impatience.

Want to know the joke of it all? We were barely late on any given Sunday because church never starts on time. Then my kids would roll their eyes and whisper to each other behind my steaming back about my 'big deal over nothing' antics. I can't stand life lessons!

I know I'm not alone in the 'losing our salvation on the way to church' club because I wrote about this once before and received a barrage of "me too" responses. So many things cause moms to be impatient: 15 outfit changes by a daughter before leaving the house to do anything, or marathon toy cleanups by preschoolers. I mean they have to play with every toy before putting the thing away, right? Which, by the way, are the same toys they complain about not having when they are bored out of their still-soft skulls. Criminy.

Or how about mad scrambles to sporting events? Those moments when you try to fast-feed your toddler before heading out the door with a family of five to a soccer game, and he decides to eat one cheerio at a time, each fully chewed before the next. Meanwhile, your soccer star is putting his shin guards on his forearms while trying to shove already chubby feet into narrow and unyielding cleats. Who designed those things?

Don't even get me started with potty time—especially when out to dinner or a movie you paid half your life's fortune to take the family to.

"Are you still poopin'??!?"

"Yeah, Momma, nofings comin' out yet."

Are they really trying to go? Let's be real. If patience is a virtue, then motherhood is a shiza show. Just sayin'. So, virtue schmirtue when it comes to foolproof tolerance.

Okay, fine. Patience is essential. I have lots. Now. It only took 21 years, which is the number between the first born and last to leave. When forbearance was on display, the self-control was only because of this (emphasis mine): *"Don't be impatient **with your children**. Wait for the Lord, and he will come and save you! Be brave, stouthearted, and courageous. Yes, wait and he will help you."* Psalm 27:14 (TLB)

While I poke fun at myself, I did have plenty of patience over the years. Just don't ask my kids.

Lisa's Reflection

I lost my cool in the check-out line at the store when one of the kids used his outstretched arm to grab hold of the magazine rack next to the cart and sent *Oprah*, *Woman's World*, and *Reader's Digest* hurtling to the ground.

I lost it again when, smack dab in the middle of our Google search for a map of Europe for the geography test we were studying for, the computer decided it deserved a work stoppage.

Let me not forget hours earlier when the toaster took so long to provide color to the bagel that I forced it to pop up before its time and burned my fingers to boot.

Mind if I mention the blue crayon marks I found on the bathtub wall that I have subsequently been informed Dad is aware of? Something about big waves taking down a ship they were searching for.

The next time I step on a Lego or stub my toe on a toy that missed the toy box I will...

(Clearing my throat)

Can you feel it?

Have you been there?

The momma is running low on patience.

No, that is definitely not an accurate assessment of current conditions.

The momma has RUN OUT of patience!

And guess what? No amount of "sorry it won't happen again" or "I didn't mean it" will cut it.

Don't go where I sense you are headed with "he started first" or "you're mean," the Mama is thinking to herself. This is 'mean-light' so don't push it!

Momma needs to leave the room and re-group.

The problem is, for most of us, we do not have the luxury of picking up a phone and requesting reinforcements. You know, like temporary substitutes who can come in and give us a break for a few minutes.

And we can't walk out and ignore the kids just because our patience has waned and we feel like it. We have to be super beings and re-group WHILE still engaged in battle.

It's a trait that moms excel at.

But boy do I wish I had the skill set to maintain my patience so I would never hit that stratospheric level of IMPATIENCE.

What do you do, Momma?

Do you breathe deeply?

Or drink the wine?

Shouldn't we collaborate on a booklet that lists our best tried and true ways of handling these times and give it as gifts to one another?

Or perhaps do what's in our power to do: chat with God. He hears us over the mayhem, and we can have our talk while still parenting the troops.

"I waited patiently for the Lord; he turned to me and heard my cry." Psalm 40:1 (NIV)

That Psalm alone has brought a sense of calm to my soul and restored order.

Then I step on another Lego piece!

Breathe, Momma, breathe.

Personal Reflection:

What challenging people or situations do you need to change your mindset about to grow in patience?

Twelve

PSALMS FOR INSECURE MOMS

Lisa's Reflection

What is it in our make-up that causes us to rely upon others to validate our worth?

Why do our lives always revolve around questions like, "Am I good enough?" or "What happens if I'm not?"

I ask, "What happens if you are?"

There are a few conditions about motherhood that likely will not change if you checked back 1,000 years from now.

Mothers should not expect to receive accolades for providing top-notch quality services. There are no annual awards ceremonies honoring great mom accomplishments.

No one is going to write you a check for over-time.

The list goes on and on and on.

If we wait for someone other than ourselves to express value about ourselves, we will wander longer than Moses did in the desert.

It turns out that every mom I've met suffers from (drum roll, please) I N S E C U R I T Y!

What's up with that anyway?

How dare we feel insecure about performing a job that would have to be divided up among at least 20 employees daily, and that's only to nip the surface.

If you want it done right, I think we're talking close to 40.

It's frustrating to hear that moms battle with self-doubts so often.

Stop for a second and consider what God must have been thinking when He designed us. He must have thought the world of us or else why create a being who can carry and support other human beings both on the inside and out? That's darn remarkable folks! Beyond remarkable. It's mind-blowing!

So how about we make a pact to go on a mission to change the message we subscribe to?

Here's how the mantra might sound:

"We are worth our weight in Gold."

"We are permitted to make mistakes without jeopardizing our worth and causing us to feel insecure."

"Insecurity in small to medium doses is distracting."

"Insecurity in medium to high doses is toxic."

"I will change my inner voice to honor myself and the women around me."

Perhaps a wise woman who came well before all of us (even me) said it best:

"No one can make you feel inferior without your consent."

That was Eleanor Roosevelt's mantra.

How about we make it ours?

"For he will command his angels concerning you to guard you in all your ways." Psalm 91:11 (NIV)

Shelby's Reflection

Lisa and I have never met in person. Our friend affair is all cyber and cell tower based. From my writing alone, and conversations via email, text, and phone, this Jewish sage picked up that I'm insecure, and in the kindest and most gentle way possible, told me so.

Seriously? How does she know? Why does she think this? Do I sound insecure? Do I come across wrong? Are my words offensive? Do I sound needy? How about ignorant? Does she think my messages are askew? Maybe I should stop writing? Do I even know what I'm doing?

These are a few of the questions I've tossed into the cloud during our two-year pen pal connection. I still have no idea why Lisa thinks I'm insecure. Pf. But, alas, turns out I am. The spade is on the table. Especially in mothering.

I wanted to be *the BEST* at mothering. I made a bajillion personal promises about all the ways I'd ensure my kids had a serene upbringing, free of trauma, drama, and any mistakes or misgivings on my part. This coupled with a personal pledge to be confident and secure in raising our family.

Well, my pledge lasted about three days, which is when I realized I didn't know crapola about what was the right thing to do, let alone the best thing, as a mother. Thank God for instinct. No, really God, thanks. But could you have vacuum packed the convenience of acting on impulse inside 100% certainty? We mothers constantly second-guess our parenting decisions and measure our kid's successes and failures alongside the growth charts penciled on other mom's walls. Oh, the drama of it all. And waste of energy.

Lest you think empty nesting numbs the qualms, never think such nonsense again. Big kids are synonymous with big problems, and big problems synonymous with big doubts about all past and present mothering decisions. I daydream of the days when my uncertainty hinged on whether letting my kids play or not play travel sports was the right thing to do.

I've come to accept we mostly almost always don't know what we are doing. Our only hope for feeling certain security is in God. In Him we raise our kids to the best of our ability, trusting His guidance over our mental bartering. Trying to do the Mom thing on our own accord is fool's play. God knows. We don't. These are His kids. Not ours. He gave us this job because He thinks we can do it. Our insecurity questions His wisdom. Goodness gracious, I have put Him to the test.

Just like a toddler testing the weaning from his mother, we can try with all our might to go it alone. But chances are, our best bet is to run like an unsure child back to our Father and get the squeeze of encouragement and earful of instruction we need. I like to think the 'in' in the word insecurity really means 'in (Him), security abounds.'

"Teach me how to live, O Lord. Lead me along the path of honesty, for my enemies are waiting for me to fall." Psalm 27:11 (NLT)

Personal Reflection:

Name your greatest insecurities and ask God to help you grow in confidence and strength.

Thirteen

PSALMS FOR INSULTED MOMS

Shelby's Reflection

My kids have bowed back and let some colorful words soar toward me over the years. My daughter's coveted phrase at five-years-old was, "I hate you," and my middle son declared, "I only want to spend time with Daddy," when he was three. Ouch! And my oldest, at 13, told me, "I believe her word over yours," when referring to his girlfriend's mother. That went over not well.

If another word for insulted is offended, then I've been both, too many times to count. No one likes to have their soul scathed. As moms, we not only feel jaded by our kids sometimes, but we can feel cored by things said by our family members, other moms, and friends. In the social media world, insulting comments from total strangers can be a gut punch. I don't know what's worse, having shade thrown at us from someone who really knows our heart or taking an emotional beating via impulsive assumptions from someone who doesn't know us at all.

The thing about young kids is they don't really have malice in their hearts. Growing up is hard, and spewed feelings tend to have a mind of their own. When our kiddos reach the tween and teen years, I'm pretty sure fire and brimstone (in the form of whacked out hormones, immaturity, and ignorance) is the launching pad of many of their insults. We've all been there on one side or the other (or both).

But adulting is different. As a general rule, I don't make a point of trying to offend someone. Unfortunately, I have indeed hurt people with my words and assumptions over the years. On the flip side, I've taken things personally when, more times than not, the person making the statement didn't intend harm.

One of my favorite books is *The Four Agreements: A Practical Guide to Personal Freedom* by Don Miguel Ruiz. This single book changed the way my spouse, our kids, and I approach both sides of the communication realm. I don't have enough space in this reflection to do the value of the message justice, but I encourage all of you to read the book. If we can put into practice any/all of these agreements, we will offend fewer people and feel less offended.

1. **Be Impeccable with your Word**

Use the power of your word in the direction of truth and love.

2. **Don't Take Anything Personally**

Nothing others do is because of you. What others say and do is a projection of their own reality. When you are immune to the opinions and actions of others, you won't be the victim of needless suffering.

3. **Don't Make Assumptions**

Find the courage to ask questions and to express what you really want. Communicate with others as clearly as you can to avoid misunderstandings, sadness, and drama.

4. **Always Do Your Best**

Your best is going to change from moment to moment; the results will be different when you are healthy as opposed to sick. Under any circumstance, simply do your best, and you will avoid self-judgment, self-abuse, and regret.

"While they curse, may you bless.; may those who attack me be put to shame, but may your servant rejoice." Psalm 109:28 (NIV)

Lisa's Reflection

I unwittingly insulted a beautiful young mother the other day when I shared some mom advice without being asked.

We were at the park, and she was trying to corral a defiant three-year-old off the slide and into the car.

I did my "sometimes if you..." impression and though she graciously smiled and replied, "That's a good idea," I heard the hurt and realized what I had done.

In an effort to be helpful, I had actually demeaned this mother by inserting myself into her problem, as if she could not manage it.

Though my words were intended as a gesture of outreach, she heard a judgment no different than if I had said, "You're not handling this properly. Here's a better way."

Sometimes when we mean the best, we are causing more harm, adding fuel to an already volatile situation.

When it comes to mothering, we walk through trenches daily.

I have discovered that many moms will reach out and ask for insight and guidance if they are navigating a trench you have already survived.

When they do, give freely.

When they don't, and they are merely expressing their frustrations, LISTEN, SMILE, HUG.

But zippy the lippy.

Too many times, words of advice can insult rather than lift the ones we love!

"I said, 'Have mercy on me, LORD; heal me, for I have sinned against you.'" Psalm 41:4 (NIV)

Personal Reflection:

Do you struggle with taking things personally or making assumptions? Spend the next few days keeping track.

Fourteen

PSALMS FOR JEALOUS MOMS

Lisa's Reflection

The Green Monster rears his ugly head again.

We are gathered at a local bistro to have a few appetizers and a few laughs while the kids stay home with a cadre of loved ones from husbands to grandparents to aunts to special grownups.

It's a 'try and schedule time with some Moms in your neighborhood without the kids' gathering that occurs as irregularly as sex after children.

I am seated across from a mother who is so well put together I assume she has a standing hair salon appointment.

MY nails are chipped and cracked and have a patina from years of old polish.

Her fashion is so trendy that "Project Runway" contestants probably consulted her for advice.

ME, I am grateful that my shirt does not have the sweet potato stain from last night's spit-up.

She laughs with her head back, as if she has not a care in the world.

I sneak peeks at my cell phone, sure that my kids have outsmarted the sitter and locked her in the basement.

When she talks, it's about her plans to cruise through Europe.

I am trying to drive my car to the mall without getting caught in traffic.

She knows what 'vichyssoise' is when it comes up in conversation.

I know where to get the best pea soup, so there!

She raves about her husband's job.

We are barely making ends meet on our austerity budget.

Yep, the Green Monster has taken hold and threatens to do what he does best: blind us so we lose sight of our own joy and the beauty of our lives, and drive us to compare our existence to somebody else's without knowing any of the details of theirs.

Jealously forces us to expend useless energy that lands us in a trench laden with bitterness and resentment.

The bitterness and resentment festers and threatens to consume our gratitude.

THAT mother stands up to leave.

I bet she goes to the Coat Room to claim her cashmere jacket.

A gentleman walks in to escort her out, probably her chauffeur.

Postscript:

The mother I was so jealous over was on her way back to the hospital to sit with her dying father. Her husband had insisted that she take a few hours to herself after not leaving her father's side for days.

The Green Monster distorted my perceptions and nearly stole a piece of my soul had I let him.

Don't let that happen to you.

Rejoice in all the little things you have, and remember that someone is looking at you and thinking you are incredibly blessed.

"The Lord is my shepherd; I have all that I need." Psalm 23:1 (NLT)

Shelby's Reflection

Why does she...

- get to be a SAHM
- get to be a working mom
- have better friends
- have well-behaved kids
- get the beauty gene
- get the promotion
- pray so eloquently
- have life so easy
- always seem put together
- have such a helpful hubby
- lose the weight
- have healthy *and* problem-free children?

The grass is always a deeper shade of jade in another mom's yard when we wear the glasses of comparison. Why, as moms, do we fall into the trap of covetousness? We so often long for more, or less, or equal, or different than what's right in front of us. "Why isn't," as a wise friend once said, "all we ever have enough?" Instead of feeling content with what God's given us, we bemoan,

"I'm still carrying around 17 lbs. and she bounced back to a size two after a week!"

"Her kid sleeps all night and mine's had colic for months."

"My son still wets the bed at three years old, and her kid was potty-trained at 18 months."

"She can pull off a messy bun and no make-up, and I look like death most days."

"Her kids are so talented, and mine are struggling just to read."

But aren't the above scenarios really about us? As in, something must be wrong with who we are or how we do things:

I'm not losing the weight because I'm not trying hard enough.

My kid has colic because I must be eating improper foods.

My son wets the bed because I don't know how to train him well enough.

She looks pretty, no matter what, and I was just born ugly.

Her kids have all the smarts, and mine struggle because I don't spend enough time teaching them.

How can we flip the script and fill the self-love tank? Do you think if we believed God gave us everything we need for our journey, nothing more nothing less, confidence and contentment would fill our heart space? The irony of feeling "less than" is that while we are feeling envy towards 20 other women, there are, no doubt, 100 other moms feeling jealousy towards us. Round and round the hamster wheel we scamper until we love ourselves and are satisfied with our portion—right where we are, as is.

Rumi challenges us with this axiom, "*Wherever you stand, be the soul of that place.*" If we embody our motherhood vocation—all in, full of love to the best of our ability, accepting the good and the bad, we become the incarnation of grace in that place. Nothing can diminish, degrade, deplete, or devalue the essence of our being, because the seat of the soul is where God rests. God is jealous for us too. For our affection, devotion, trust. But this is Holy envy—God longing for His image within us to meld and become besties with His greater everything.

Lord, help us to only be jealous for you, vigilant in our love and appreciation for all you give, without a desire for anything more.

"*When you open your hand, you satisfy the hunger and thirst of every living thing.*" Psalm 145:16 (NLT)

Personal Reflection:

If you find yourself in the comparison trap, reflect on the gifts, talents, and blessings God has given you.

Fifteen

PSALMS FOR MOMS WHO FEEL LIKE QUITTING

Shelby's Reflection

If mom perseverance is akin to the length of a cat's existence, then I must have way more than nine lives. Trust me when I tell you, I don't always land on my feet. The number of times I've felt like quitting as a mom? Are we talking in one day? An hour? A week? Good grief. I wanted to give up many a season.

How about you? Ever thrown your arms in the air, stormed off, threatened to purchase a one-way ticket to Antarctica? What about high tailing it in your car, heading nowhere fast?

Well, I did hop in my car back in 2007 when my kids were 13, 11, and 9. Let's just say teenagerdom didn't waltz into our family wearing a tux. We got a lot of things wrong with our oldest. God bless all first-borns for being the trial and error group.

One night, when my "I am a capable mother" meter dropped into the red zone, I packed a bag and blazed a trail to a condo we owned three hours away. On my way out the door, I mumble-yelled some nonsense to my husband, mostly accusing him of having no idea how hard mothering was, along with a threat to never return home. I still get all the feels thinking about this story, being one of my finer moments and all.

During the drive, I role-played in my narcissistic head about how apologetic my hubby would be when he called later and how sad my kids would be when they realized how much they took me for granted. But alas, once I got to my destination, the only thing greeting me was silence. No call of remorse from the spouse or kids. Turns out God was teaching me a lesson, one He shared about three hours into my self-imposed, dramatic time-out. These were His words:

"In general, I'm not a fan of you running off like a fool, but one of the perks of you loving me is me loving you right where you're at. In case you didn't know, I know people who know people. Angels, to be exact. When moms feel like quitting, I send a cloud of witnesses in full force. Did you sense them? Ah, yes you did because I saw your jaw drop and tears fall from your eyes after coming across the scripture I fixed your gaze upon when you opened your Bible.

And you know the video you watched earlier with Dallas Willard, Max Lucado, Beth Moore and others called, *Be Still*? Well, the whole point was to clarify you are still going to be a wife and mother. Running away doesn't solve anything. In your case, the short respite was good. Really good. This alone time reminded you motherhood is your calling, and I don't call the equipped, I equip the called. It's okay to feel like quitting, I get it. I can make a hard case on paper for wanting to throw in the Holy towel on humanity. The whole ungratefulness, selfishness, rudeness, pride, pettiness, and unforgiveness thing. Sigh. Children can be taxing. But I don't give up because I AM. I don't want you to give up either, because you are mine. Steady wins the race. One heavy foot in front of the other if that's what surviving takes—with me by your side at every step."

"The LORD Helps the fallen and lifts up those bent beneath their loads." Psalm 145:14 (NLT)

Lisa's Reflection

Feel like quitting?

If you're a mom, you've probably had that thought on numerous occasions, perhaps daily.

Here's the problem.

We can't quit.

Not allowed.

So what choices are there when we're in the throes of motherhood and FEEL LIKE QUITTING?

1. Breathe

Of course, we are doing this on autopilot, yet somehow if we consciously focus on our breathing, it can calm us and center us. There are scientific explanations, but who has time for them? Focus on hearing yourself breathe in and out, and if you can stand in front of a mirror for a second or two, watch your chest expand and deflate. Inhale, exhale. CAUTION: Do not fall asleep standing up. Of course that's a silly thought. A screaming baby and a toddler are tugging your kneecap. No worries there!

2. Suck on an ice cube

The immediate change in temperature causes minor physiological changes (again, a great scientific explanation awaits you, just not here) that are at once pleasant and distracting.

Any newborn would tell you that sucking anything is soothing. No different for the mommas.

If one cube is not sufficient, suck again.

We need hydration to keep us afloat, which we generally overlook, so it helps with that, too!

If you would like to add some snazz and pizazz, you can make the cubes with a variety of flavors like cranberry juice cubes (bladder benefits), or orange juice cubes (potassium or sugar boost), or perhaps lemon-lime cubes which make you pucker, and then it makes your kids laugh because they think you're making a funny face. Keep re-stocking the ice trays if your refrigerator does not come equipped with an icemaker.

3. Go to the bathroom

Not because nature calls, which we all know we never heed THAT call at the time it calls. Most of us are "hold it in until we are ready to burst" mommas by necessity. Go there to run cold water on your face and your hands. If you have the bambinos with you, sit them safely on the floor with some plastic toys and juice boxes.

And ready? Get in the bathtub.

That's right, the bathtub with your clothes on (no slippers or socks or shoes). Pretend you have been granted time to luxuriate in a bubble bath (I know this is the stuff dreams are made of). Lay your head back, stretching your sore aching neck muscles, which hopefully will feel good.

Put your legs out in front of you and wiggle your toes. Watching your toes wiggle seems silly and is kind of fun. Try sticking one of your toes in the faucet like Julia Roberts did in *Pretty Woman*. It will make you think of the movie, which will take your focus off your trench and make you think of hers. Plus she was singing at the time, which leads us to our next technique.

4. Sing

Any song as loud as you can so that your kids look at you like you've lost your mind, which you're close to doing anyway, so might as well make it worthwhile. Singing is self-entertainment, and you don't have to be Barbra Streisand. If you can do a little toe-tapping accompaniment or a little soft shoe or some finger snapping, go and jazz it up a bit. Think "American Idol" in your living room. Got a hairbrush handy? Then you've got your childhood microphone to capture the glorious melodies!

5. Hum

Humming is cursing without getting caught. I actually hum the bad words in lieu of spewing, and everyone around me thinks I am feeling joyful, and then they act joyful, and that makes me actually feel joyful, and I'm not stuck in the muck. Until the next moment…

Breathe, Momma. Breathe.

"*The LORD gives strength to his people; the LORD blesses his people with peace.*" Psalm 29:11 (NIV)

Personal Reflection:

Where can you turn for inspiration to persevere when you feel like giving up?

Sixteen

PSALMS FOR LOST MOMS

Lisa's Reflection

Car keys get lost.

People get lost trying to follow directions to a new place.

But moms? They're not supposed to get lost.

But they do, every day.

And we do not hear their cries, for they do not cry out loud. It's a silent cry.

Or if you listen very carefully, a whimper might escape. We hear the whimper. We question it.

The mom denies it was anything important, and we believe her.

DON'T BELIEVE HER!

The 'lost' mom needs a friend. She is floundering on her best days. Drowning on her worst.

Why don't we hear about the 'Lost Moms'? They are not a tribe unto themselves.

They are me.

They are you.

They are the neighbors we wave to.

They are the moms of our kids' classmates in the drop-off line at school.

They are the school bus drivers transporting our treasures to their destinations.

They are the teachers who compassionately educate.

The counselors who generously comfort.
The ones who push swings at the park, well past dusk.
And catch kids at the bottom of slides.
The same ones sewing Halloween costumes.
And making hiding spots for Christmas presents.
They are YOU!
They are ME!
They are US!
'Lost' moms on some days. Not necessarily all days.
Yet on those some days, we need one another.
But the only way to reach out is to REACH OUT!

Let us know you need us. That's what we're here for. We're warriors.

And when we're called to battle to find a 'lost' one, we take our mission seriously.

Like the military motto adjusted for gender: "No Mom Left Behind."

"Turn to me and be gracious to me, for I am lonely and afflicted. Relieve the troubles of my heart and free me from my anguish." Psalm 25:16-17 (NIV)

Shelby's Reflection

I lost myself in motherhood for sure. The minute my first son looked up at me was when God hit my heart out of the park. Going. Going. Gone. Ba-bye, any part of me I thought I knew or understood.

At first, feeling lost in motherhood was bliss. Nothing else mattered except the precious human in front of me. Well, sleep was a close second. Going back to work was brutal. My high-powered corporate accounting job didn't mesh with my heart mush. So I took a part-time opportunity with one of my firm's clients to better balance my roles. Then boy two came along, and I did a deeper dive into the abyss of raising two kids. They were my world around which I revolved, helped in part by my employer allowing me to work from home.

A blink later, daughter arrived—making the kid count three in 3 ½ years. I wanted nothing more than to be a full-time mom, and God obliged by blessing my hubby with an amazing job, earning enough to sustain our family on one income. Staying home with all three was a "Gilligan's Island" experience. I loved every minute, until I didn't.

I loved my kids to no end, but feeling lost had a new twist now. Living a life "lost in motherhood" left me feeling lost as a person. The Shelby I once knew was incognito. My identity was missing. Sure, I was Mom, but was I anybody else?

Looking back, I am forever grateful for all I've lost over the years. During the moment, the isolation overwhelmed me. The emptiness consumed me. It's difficult to see value in confusion while we are in the throes of entanglement. But although my identity once was lost, my children helped me work my way back to find the whole of me. Amazing Grace. These are the treasures God revealed over the years:

- I lost my independence but found my freedom
- I lost my energy but found my drive
- I lost my youthfulness but found my stamina
- I lost my inner mojo but found a deeper moxie
- I lost my mind but found my sanity
- I lost my patience but found my endurance
- I lost my astuteness but found my awareness
- I lost my purpose, but found my calling

In the end, I lost a lot, but I found what sticks. The residue is what matters most. Motherhood will always have its wilderness seasons. Sometimes feeling lost can be scary, depressing, overwhelming. But, I'm here to encourage all moms to let things play out. Even when you don't know which end is up, what direction to turn, or how to find your way out of the identity crisis, God is leading you on a path to wholeness, truth, and authenticity. He uses your children to help get you there. Disorientation is natural. Unfolding is cleansing. Transformation is healing. Finding is everything.

By finding, I mean finding God. Our identities can take on many forms: mother, wife, sister, daughter, employee, neighbor, friend. But when we find out who we are in Christ by identifying with His presence within us, we find what's true and authentic.

"You chart the path ahead of me and tell me where to stop and rest. Every moment you know where I am." Psalm 139:3 (NLT)

Personal Reflection:

Has there been a time God helped you find your way when you were feeling lost?

Seventeen

PSALMS FOR OVERWHELMED MOMS

Shelby's Reflection

As moms, ensuring the health, safety, and well-being of our children is only one enormous responsibility we have in life. Other roles may include wife, volunteer, career person, caregiver, confidant, ministry leader, coach, etc. When so many moving parts vie for our attention, the load can be overwhelming. At any given moment, one or more of these areas can break down and leave us reeling.

If we don't tend to the damage when the mishaps occur, before long our life as a whole can get out of hand. I've been there. When my house was full of littles, my husband traveled for work. Over time, my exhaustion turned to resentment, which gave birth to marital strife, which resulted in sleepless nights. During the teen years, the battles over independence left me frazzled, which morphed into eating stress for breakfast, lunch, and dinner, which brewed up ulcers in my belly.

What I've come to learn the hard way is the value and importance of slowing down, to pause long enough to take a step back and evaluate what's going on. Sometimes this looks like getting away for a day by myself, meeting up with supportive friends, or making the time to attend a weekend spiritual retreat. Getting away from the noise in our head so we can be alone with God does wonders. We can usually hear Him speak to our situation when we allow ourselves the freedom to listen.

If you've never heard the name Bob Goff, you'll want to earmark this page, underline this sentence, and get a highlighter out. He is love personified and the author of two amazing books, *Love Does* and *Everybody Always*. In a recent interview[6], Bob said something that resonated deep within me. In referencing moments in life when we feel stuck, overwhelmed, underwhelmed, unmotivated, etc., he suggested we think of a bottle of wine aging in a cellar. Every month, the vintner needs to rotate the bottle a quarter turn (called riddling) to ensure displacement of the sediments spread across the bottom length of the bottle. This is what ensures the clarity of the wine.

Bob made the analogy of how when we get into ruts, doldrums, or seasons of exasperation; we also need to make a quarter turn in our life to release the muck settled in our hearts, thus enabling us to move in a healthier direction.

While I wish I would have heard his sage advice decades ago, I feel like I've implemented a lighter version of the quarter turn along the way by scheduling time for myself.

I pray you can do the same and more with God by your side. Not until then do we see with clarity how to get back on track. God longs for us to tend to whatever steals our peace, which begins by rooting ourselves in Him.

"I pour out my complaints before him and tell him all my troubles. When I am overwhelmed, and you alone know the way I should turn." Psalm 142:2-3 (NLT)

Lisa's Reflection

One poopy diaper
Two poopy diapers
Three poopy diapers four.
The U.P.S. man is at the door.

---

6 Lewis Howes School of Greatness Podcast Ep 622: Bob Goff, Love Everyone Always

How Are You Feeling, Momma?

The Dog started barking
One toddler got mad
The other is screaming,
"My brother is bad."

The baby was napping
Until the first toddler said,
"I was sharing my Legos
But they fell on his head."

There's not one clean utensil
It's cheese sticks for lunch
And Dinner? A Pizza?
That is my hunch.

The hubby is calling with questions for me
He must be insane to think I can answer with three.

I feel something sticky
Attach to my arm.
The Middle found glue sticks
I guess there's no harm.

The baby spit up all the contents and more
Do you believe my neighbor is now at the door?

What's wrong with these people?
Must I post a sign?
"Do not disturb me until they are nine"!

Have you seen a shower?
Drank a coffee that's hot?
Put up your feet
I know that's a NOT!

You're a mom, so it goes without saying, I think

There is no time to breathe, and the stress level stinks.

We HEAR you. We FEEL you.
We share the same trench.
Overwhelmed and exhausted
In search of a bench.

Yet we all try to bear it
For the day comes so fast.
When they're waving goodbye
And we know that's our last.

"From the ends of the earth, I cry to you for help when my heart is overwhelmed. Lead me to the towering rock of safety." Psalm 61:2 (NLT)

Personal Reflection:

Reflect on how you can simplify your life or tend to an issue, and then implement the plan.

Eighteen
PSALMS FOR PENITENT MOMS

Lisa's Reflection

On behalf of women everywhere may I say sorry Momma for the times we sat here and judged you from our ivory towers?

Going public with these private admonishments shames me into saying sorry one million times more.

Your children's noses are always running! Why don't you bring tissues?

How come you allow your children to stay up late and do not adhere to a standard bedtime? Haven't you read that children require a certain amount of sleep each night?

You let your children drink soda? That is so irresponsible!

Isn't one and a half a bit too old for breastfeeding? He barely fits in your lap.

Your child is hidden behind his video screen longer than his face is buried in a textbook. Don't you monitor what he is doing?

I never heard your child say "please" and "thank you." My children were taught to have manners.

Why is your child on a skateboard without a helmet? Are you not concerned about a concussion?

Your children are always talking in church. Why don't you tell them to stop?

Judgments.

Rude comments mumbled under our breath.

Rolled eyes at the other moms in our sisterhood.

Tsk-tsks.

Ivory towers.

Then the inevitable plummet from the golden perch when WE become Mommas.

And there is not a tissue in sight, nor did we think to bring any.

We're barely hanging on to a rope about to unleash.

Sorry, Momma.

We never knew.

We do now.

Please forgive us.

"Praise be to God, who has not rejected my prayer or withheld his love from me!" Psalm 66:20 (NIV)

Shelby's Reflection

Anyone enjoy being the cause of their kid's feelings of sadness, frustration, hurt, disappointment, fear, anger, or sorrow? I'm guessing the answer is a hard 'no' because the last thing we want is to be the source of our child's negative experience. But sometimes we are, and those moments are the worst. The remorse can keep us awake for days—a separate topic we discussed earlier, the mom guilt phenomenon.

My mothering history includes countless examples of times I've apologized to my kiddos for being a bonehead, jerk, crazed maniac, forgetful hearer, unavailable comforter, disrespectful wordsmith, embarrasser, ignorer, etc. While the sheer number of regret-worthy scenarios still leaves me scratching my heart, the good news is I found the resolve within myself in those moments to say, "I'm sorry."

Those two words mean everything to a child. Kids are super forgiving by nature, and admitting our wrongs melds well with their grace offerings. Modeling accountability has a forever impact on our children. When we royally screw up as a mom but then have enough courage and self-love to overcome the shame and apologize, our kids learn it's okay to be human, i.e., not perfect.

Expressing our regret lets our kid know we value and respect their feelings—whether the severity of what we did is significant (freaked out on them in front of their peers) or minuscule (forgot to pick up essential school supplies on the way home from work). Hurt is hurt and deserves a healing salve of "I hear you. I see you. I pray you can forgive me."

Aside from apologizing to the person we've wronged, what if we say sorry to ourselves as well? God designed us in His image, which means love defines our core. By nature, love doesn't offend. So when we make a mistake and hurt another person, a side of us that isn't genuine committed the wrong. Yet, self-bashing and mom guilt are unfair strongholds we cast over our transgressions. The sooner we can accept our children and, God forgive us, the sooner we can forgive ourselves so we can be the love we're made of.

"Finally, I confessed all my sins to you and stopped trying to hide my guilt. I said to myself, "I will confess my rebellion to the LORD." And you forgave me! All my guilt is gone." Psalm 32:5 (NLT)

Personal Reflection:

Who do you need to apologize to and why?

Nineteen

PSALMS FOR PRIDEFUL MOMS

Shelby's Reflection

As humiliating as it is for me to admit, pride is often my nemesis when it comes to motherhood. Not because I like to boast about my kids or think they can do no wrong. Especially not because I think I'm some kind of fail-proof mother. Rather, my penchant for pride is a subtle belief that somehow I know better than God what is best for my kids—an attitude which insists I need to take things into my own hands when it comes to solving problems, giving guidance, and protecting my kids from the harsh realities of life. Pride in my world is synonymous with control.

But the root of my need to control is really fear. Fear of bad things happening on my watch, which drives me to try and usurp God's authority. As if.

The late Wayne Dyer is a blessing to me. I love his heart and wisdom. One of the biggest lessons I learned from him years ago is an acronym for the word ego: Edge God Out. I've never forgotten this concept, except for when I do because, pride. When we think our influence on our kids' experience reigns supreme, then we are edging God out of His rightful place in our kids' lives. The end game is debilitating anxiety when life doesn't roll the way we hope and expect.

Trust me when I say the anxiety I've endured because of my stubborn will to control has only served to steal my joy. I've missed out on precious 'now' moments in my obsessive pursuit to control future outcomes. But I press on towards the goal of trust and surrender the best I can, even if it's four steps forward and two steps back—crying out to God along the way.

"Do not let not the foot of pride come near me. Do not let the hand of the sinful push me away." Psalm 36:11 (NLV)

Lisa's Reflection

I think there ought to be a 'Boastful Mom' day.

As neighbors sharing the same trench in 'Stuck in the Muck' Boulevard, perhaps sharing prideful moments might temporarily distract us from the yucky ones.

I'll go first:

I am incredibly proud of ME!

That's right! You heard it here first.

Bet you thought I was going to list all my kids' glorious achievements from the first word through potty training—kindergarten graduation through honor rolls, learning permits through college acceptance letters!

No, no and triple no!

I am going to boast about MY prideful achievements:

1. I got up this morning! Yes, I did. I did not wish to since I was still up at 4 a.m. cleaning poop off a crib and chasing a boogeyman in the room across the hall.

2. I drank a cold cup of coffee without grimacing, gagging or complaining. This particular cup survived six microwaved lives without turning to sludge.

3. I found a clean shirt UNDER the laundry basket that did not have a stain on, near, or next to a boob AND (wait for it) I PUT it on! Okay, I did not have the energy to fetch the deodorant. However, clean is clean!

4. I got the kids to the bus stop BEFORE the bus left. And might I add with backpacks, lunch boxes and homework assignments not left behind on the kitchen counter (alright, one lone permission slip lost its way).

5. I ran the shower. I didn't say I actually stepped in and took one, yet the intention was there. Then the baby spit up, and all bets were off.

6. I picked up the kids from the bus stop BEFORE the bus left the curb! I'm on a genuine roll here after a hectic night and a hectic morning and an afternoon of laundry, dishes, burping, poopy diapers, nosy neighbors, laundry, dishes, burping, poopy diapers (I seem to be repeating myself).

7. I remembered all my children's names, made sure everyone had something on their dinner plates, found cool leftover treats from Grandma to use as homework and bedtime bribe material, got everyone bubble-bathed, cuddled, snuggled, *'Good Night Moon'ed'* and left time to make sure everyone heard an, "I love you for so many reasons," loud and clear. The last one I leave the most time for and I am the proudest of, particularly when I walk out of their rooms to the glorious sounds of, "I love you more!"

"Thank you for making me so wonderfully complex! Your workmanship is marvelous—and how well I know it." Psalm 139:14 (NLT)

Personal Reflection:

In what way do you try to control? Do you love yourself enough to believe your best is good enough, and are you willing to let God do the rest?

Twenty
PSALMS FOR PURPOSELESS MOMS

Lisa's Reflection

You know the phrase "running around like a chicken without a head"?

That was invented after seeing me aimlessly wandering from room to room and not making any headway in my daily mom life.

Laundry has not only spilled beyond its basket barriers, but it has also created a walking minefield where you have to step around and over and left and right until you make it to the only open space in the house (by the fridge).

Dishes are stacked (not in the clean dishpan). They are piled in the sink by hubby who was apparently trying to locate a clean spoon and had to create a space to search.

The baby's high chair has crusted sweet potato on its legs.

The toddler's crib has a sheet with spit-up stains right on Dora's map.

If a vacuum cleaner company wanted to make a commercial using those little dust bunnies to demonstrate effective sucking motion, our living room would certainly make a good choice.

What am I doing with my life that nothing seems to get accomplished?

What progress have I made?

If I look around and use what I see as a measuring stick, then the answer is sadly 'not much.'

My house is a mess.

My hair is hanging in limp strands.

I have not returned a phone call from a friend in weeks.

What's my purpose here anyway?

Am I a dismal failure?

HOLD the PHONE!

What is wrong with me?

Am I standing in judgment of myself?

I AM A MOTHER!

There is no higher purpose on this earth, and if I doubt that, then I ought to think about what God has to say about mothers.

He thinks we are AMAZING creatures!

We are!

Even though we appear to be wandering aimlessly, we are busy building lives through LOVING and being role models and creating pathways for successful journeys.

None of these aforementioned activities is visible and quantifiable in standard terms.

Purposeless?

Not on your life!

"Teach us to number our days, that we may gain a heart of wisdom!" Psalm 90:12 (NIV)

Shelby's Reflection

"For the past six months, I've been struggling with this emptiness—this feeling that I'm not doing something worthy with my life. I long for fulfillment and am searching for answers. What is my purpose in this life?"

The above is my journal entry from November 11, 1998, one year after a transition to SAHM from a full-time Big 6 corporate accounting position. I went from wearing suits and eating fancy lunches to spending my days wearing t-shirts and sweats covered in peanut butter and spit-up. Weeks once filled with challenging spreadsheet analysis and account reconciliations now included Barney sing-a-longs, diaper changes, and endless kitchen cleanups.

The contrast left me reeling for a time, even though I wanted this life. I desired nothing more than to quit my job and be home with my precious babes. Their love for me and mine for them fueled me, but not enough to fill my soul space around purpose.

As I read the words in my journal, I am shocked by my confession. It's so apparent now that the purpose I longed for 20 years ago was staring me in the face. But as a young Mom living in a world where job status meant something for a woman, I presumed leaving my career to mother at home meant I no longer wielded the intelligence or capability to hang with the big wigs. The whispers of society told me staying home dumbed me down.

Through wise counsel, prayer, a loving spouse, and encouraging, Godly friends, I learned to rewrite the script. When I shifted my focus to loving my kids well and serving them each day, my purpose came into focus. According to Jesus, loving and serving are what this whole human journey is about. The two-fold action is to be the real driving force underlying everything we do in life. Regardless of our current role, job, duty, responsibility, the purpose stays the same:

- As a wife, we love and serve our spouse
- As a mom, we love and serve our children
- As a volunteer, we love and serve our community
- As a friend, we love and serve our relationships
- As a worker, we love and serve our clients
- As a writer, we love and serve our tribe
- As a coach, we love and serve our players
- As a ministry leader, we love and serve those seeking God

Love is the core of who we are—purpose is love reflected in all we are doing. Being love is Jesus' greatest commandment at work. In this mindset and heartset of love and service, we will find joy, reward, peace, healing, and fulfillment, regardless of where God plants our feet.

"The LORD will vindicate me; your steadfast love, your love, LORD, endures forever—do not abandon the works of your hands." Psalm 138:8 (NIV)

Personal Reflection:

Ask God to help you see your purpose the way He does by opening your eyes to greater truths about your calling.

Twenty-One

PSALMS FOR SAD MOMS

Shelby's Reflection

Sadness happens. We can't escape it, avoid it, or prevent it. The blues grab hold of our heart for countless reasons. But when sadness looms for our children, the emptiness feels denser. We feel sad for our kids when they:

feel left out
lose a big game
don't make the cut
fail a test after studying all night
worry about us
lose a pet
struggle with math

Our heart aches when a:

friend betrays them
girlfriend/boyfriend breaks up with them
coach ignores them
the teacher doesn't believe in them
the dream ends because of an injury

Anything causing our child to feel downhearted brings out the mourning in us. Our empathy runs deep, and we want nothing more than to take their sadness upon ourselves and relieve them of their sorrow. I'm dealing with this as a mom right now. My sadness for two of my young adult kids is ocean deep. But more times than not, we can't fix the situation. We can only love them through the agony as best we can.

The hard part for us as moms is being okay with such a limited role. As helpers and nurturers, allowing nature to take its course is maddening. Sometimes loving our kids forward seems altogether inadequate and we shake our fists at the universe, wishing we could do more.

But deep down we know disappointments make us stronger. Which is why teaching our kids how to handle despair is crucial to loving them forward. A beautiful quote by Rilke points us in the right direction, *"Trust in your heaviness, and patiently fall. This is what the bird teaches us."*

Feeling sad is another one of those crummy sidekicks of being a human. But if we can find the courage to fall into God's love through prayer and meditation, He can help us find our way again. The Psalms are full of sad hearts pleading with God for relief.

"O Lord, God of my salvation, I cry out to you by day. I come to you at night. Now hear my prayer; listen to my cry." Psalm 88:1-2 (NLT)

Lisa's Reflection

I thought I'd look forward to the day when I could…

- actually sit and finish a full cup of coffee while it is still piping HOT, not in semi-sips over a 24-hour period.
- reach into my pocketbook for one of my essentials and not have it come out stuck to a family of gummy bears.
- shower with the door wide open and step out naked as a jaybird without worrying about being ambushed by little Ninja Turtles.

- close both eyes at the same time and not have to sleep with one eye open and both my listening ears on red alert.
- lay no one else's clothing out but my own, or for that matter, stay in my birthday suit all day long.
- stop spoon-feeding macaroni & cheese like it was an airplane on a runway ready for takeoff.
- forget about cajoling friends, neighbors and perfect strangers into donating to the volleyball booster club for a team that went 0-14.
- eat a meal at the dinner table and not find broccoli and asparagus florets underneath everyone's chairs and dangling from the dog's mouth.
- do a load of laundry IF I felt like it and not because school clothes and sports uniforms blocked the entrance to our basement.
- forego the lies about Bubba the goldfish (#'s 1-15), who floated to the top of the bowl, got flushed down another bowl and were miraculously reincarnated before the bus dropped you back home.
- hang a masterpiece above the living room sofa that was not designed with Crayola crayons, gold stars, and glitter.
- let the boogeyman frolic freely, whether in the closet or under the bed or wherever he felt comfortable spending the evening.
- relegate *Good Night Moon* to the Free Library and take out a juicy and lascivious romance novel.
- win at Monopoly and hoard all the hotels, not having to pretend that when I landed on Boardwalk, it did not interest me in the least.
- watch a T.V. show (any show) without having to answer questions like "Will my 'gina get married?"
- brush my teeth without a timer present or teach gargling, which is really drooling with pleasant flavors.

- sit on the couch and snuggle with your father before being summoned to your room because your thumb tastes funny.
- leave the fake smiles behind for coaches that kept you on the sidelines for an entire season other than the two minutes of court time you were granted when the score was so lopsided it did not matter.
- talk to a girlfriend uninterrupted until HER child, not mine, said she smelled doody on her doll.

I thought I'd look forward to the day when I could do all these things and more. Then, with little or no warning that I can recall, that day arrived. There has not been one second since that moment where I would not trade in every steaming cup of hot coffee for just one more chance to read *Good-Night Moon*. (This reflection was originally published on Her View From Home)

"How long must I wrestle with my thoughts and day after day have sorrow in my heart? How long will my enemy triumph over me?" Psalm 13:2 (NIV)

Personal Reflection:

Allow yourself to feel the sadness if something is bringing you down. Then look for the way God's light is shining through the darkness.

Twenty-Two

PSALMS FOR SELF-CONFIDENT MOMS

Lisa's Reflection

When we're students in elementary school, the teacher puts a gold star on our ABC's, and it boosts our confidence.

The coach cheers for us and the bleachers erupt in collective enthusiasm when we run the bases in T-ball.

A blue ribbon is pinned to our chests in high school for our participation in a community park clean-up project.

Then there's motherhood, the one occupation in life where you're on call 24/7. No instruction manual, no training, no gold star, no cheering section. How's a momma expected to feel confident when all day, every day she's being exposed to and bombarded with comparison messages like these:

Whose child achieved what milestone when?

Whose home looks most Pinterest worthy and inviting?

Who's preparing the most healthy and nutritionally based meals for their family?

It becomes a constant battle to quell the voices residing in our minds that speak only of "mom fails." Isn't there a better way? I believe so.

Take a genuine look at the life you've created for your children.

Are they loved?

Protected?

Fed?

Clothed?
Nurtured?
Celebrated?
That's the answer! That is enough!

You're enough if you answered "yes" to the above, and that includes all the days when you fall short of perfection since perfection should not be in our vocabulary. We're our own confidence builders since no one else has stepped forward and offered to take on this gigantic role. On those days when your confidence wanes or needs a kick-start or has not shown up for duty, lean on another momma whose confidence might have been recently boosted. You get a turbo effect and can ride their fumes until yours spark once more.

"They will receive blessing from the LORD and vindication from God their Savior." Psalm 24:5 (NIV)

Shelby's Reflection

Dear Self-Confident Mom,

I admire you. Up close and from afar. I've had moments of feeling confident for sure, but fleeting sureness is more my pace. You are a rare breed and deserve mad props for inner strength. In case you weren't aware, you are a role model to the masses. We of the low self-esteem squad need someone to emulate and learn from when it comes to believing in ourselves.

Where do you get your moxie anyway? How did you find strength at such a young age while raising all these kiddos? I've seen you in action. Like at Walmart the other day. You were standing behind me in the checkout line—baby in the cart and two toddlers fidgeting around your legs. As you began unloading items onto the conveyer belt, your little ones started rummaging through the candy stacks. You gently asked them to "only look" and refrain from handling the packages.

At first, your kids obliged, but after a minute they took advantage of your distractedness and took up their hunt for the sweet stuff. Again, you spoke tender discipline, "Michael and Angela, I asked you not to touch the candy. I know everything looks fun and yummy, but I need you to listen to me."

After this, you smiled and loved up your baby while your toddlers stood on tippy-toes and strained their necks to see above the loading counter. Curiosity had the best of them. Your little boy reached up and tried to take granola bars off the belt. Meanwhile, your daughter began whimpering about needing to go potty, and the baby started fussing. True to form, you spoke to your children with grace and composure, confident and patient.

You didn't realize, but I was observing and listening the entire time. The thing is, I had a lousy morning with my teenage daughter. More like a dreadful span of days as a mom in general. I walked into Walmart with the weight of the universe on my chest, second-guessing all my mothering decisions and capabilities. I'm sure a cloud of mental anguish floated above my head as I wheeled my cart in and out of grocery aisles. I was hurting, feeling like a failure, this after 20+ years of semi-solid parenting.

But not you. You stood as a pillar of confidence, teaching with love, speaking with grace. I watched in admiration, recalling the days and even seasons when my self-esteem and mothering mojo also felt stable and secure. Oh, how I longed to feel such self-assurance now.

After I paid for my groceries, I made a point to turn to you and get your attention.

"I just want you to know what a great mom you are. I've noticed you loving on your children with patience and grace. I'd like to say thank you for making my day, but you've really made my week. God bless you."

Tears welled up in your eyes. You were so taken aback by my words, you lost your own for a moment.

"Thank you so much for saying that. I really do try!" you said with a smile.

I told you to enjoy your kiddos to the fullest and made my way out of the store. Although I walked in feeling empty, I left full of hope, all because of your example. You reminded me I really do try my best as a mom as well. Sometimes I forget how much I get right. Thank you for showing me once again that doing our best is what we moms need to build our confidence upon. This and full reliance on God. The FROG thing.

Blessings,
An admiring mom

"O my Strength, I will sing praises to You. For God is my strong place and the God Who shows me loving-kindness." Psalm 59:17 (NLV)

Personal Reflection:

List all the reasons you are a great mom. Like all of 'em, because there are a lot.

Twenty-Three

PSALMS FOR TENSE MOMS

Shelby's Reflection

Turning 40 made me want to recalibrate every aspect of my life. So as I approached the pinnacle of four decades, I did a complete inventory of my inner self: heart check, soul check, health check, mind check. Some parts were good, others so-so. Being out of physical shape fell on the not-so-good list.

The weird thing is, I had lots of muscle tone in my younger years, even when I didn't eat green leafy stuff like it's my job or bike and row myself into oblivion like I do now. But turns out the leanness was mostly a result of extreme tension—a convenient perk of stress if there ever was one. Which there isn't. Plus, I'm not a doctor or scientist, which means I am making stuff up.

What I'm not lying about is that I had an ulcer at one point when our oldest was going through a big-time struggle in the 8th grade. Too much worrying and fretting made me uptight on the regular. I couldn't relax with my mom radar on high alert—mom worry at DEFCON status and mom guilt in perpetual overdrive. Then a few years ago a different kid issue manifested into months of stomach issues and another ulcer.

All the red-level statuses kept me from winning Mom of the Year for every year running. Because you know what happens when Mom's tense, right? The whole fam damily buckles under the pressure. Tension follows us like smog. The negative energy seeps into the air around us, forcing others to inhale our distress. "Yay!" said no family member ever.

But how do we relax during times of high stress? What can we do to find peace when we are in full clench mode?

One thing I did to help myself chill out was to attend a Christ Renews His Parish women's renewal. Listening to other women share testimonies of their struggles, losses, and victories reminded me that perspective is a game changer. Leaning into others to hear their story and in turn share ours is a healing balm. Unmasking our collective tension somehow helps us all decompress.

Now eight years into the new me, I've come to accept that regular self-care is the ticket to tension relief. We've all been taught the main ingredients: healthy eating, exercise, plenty of rest. Also, regular communion with God keeps us grounded in the truth that something bigger than us exists—a power superior enough to take on the stress of all humanity.

In addition to practicing yoga several times a week, I like to say a simple mantra to start my day or calm me down when I begin to coil up:

Touch your index finger and say PEACE.
Touch your middle finger and say BEGINS.
Touch your ring finger and say WITH.
Touch your pinky finger and say ME.

I like to think the last pinky stanza continues with, "...turning to God for relief."

"When anxiety was great within me, your consolation brought me joy." Psalm 94:19 (NIV)

Lisa's Reflection

Dear Child of Mine,

I don't want you to leave my side. I mean it! Literally, not figuratively. I don't trust the world with you. Too many times the news scares the bejesus out of me. It's sometimes hard to take a deep breath.

While you're sleeping, it sometimes rests too, and then I start thinking and BOOM! Sabbatical over! I am trying carefully not to allow my tenseness to seep into your life, however keeping it under wraps is becoming a full-time job. I scour women's magazines for tension-reducing exercises. I ask other mommas what they do to cope. One thing is certain: Mommas have tension overload verging on cray cray!

Here's my new regimen that I have designed to address my tenseness:

1. **BREATHING**

I'm not referring to the type that occurs naturally. I mean consciously attending to my breathing like they do in yoga class to try and calm the nerves. Slow and steady. In and out. Through the nose and out the mouth. What's great is that I can concentrate on this technique while in the throes of motherhood. Cautionary note: no deep breathing while changing poopy diapers.

2. **LOW-CALORIE SNACKING**

I easily orally fixate. That's probably why I'm in and out of chubby my entire life. When tense, I'm inclined to seek chocolate. It's such a glorious tension reliever. My new plan entails grabbing crunchy celery sticks (dipped in peanut butter), honey wheat pretzels (dipped in peanut butter) and water bottles (to wash down the peanut butter stuck to the roof of my mouth). And the occasional Hershey Kiss as a reward for sticking to my newly acquired low-calorie snacking.

3. **HOMEBOUND EXERCISE**

Mommas don't have the luxury of leaving the house on demand. Joining a gym class? A futile fairy tale for most of us. So I create my own exercise routine right in the heart of the home. Walking the hallway back and forth 11x's (with a baby on my back), coupled with 25 leg lifts while seated on the couch (with a toddler on my lap), combined with 20 rug sit-ups (the kids think it's hilarious and there's an extra benefit because they try to copy me) is the basis for a fairly decent workout routine. Of course, we need to be flexible because the kid's routines come first. Did you know that you can shake your booty while heating up chicken nuggets and burn approximately 35 calories per serving?

4. **CHATTING WITH GOD MORE OFTEN**

This might be the best advice I offer myself and every other momma. We can chat with God everywhere; in carpool lanes, at the bus stop, while cheering on our kids in the bleachers, at the PTA pancake breakfast, and even during diaper changes. These diaper chats have always delivered results. I've discovered that like every loving momma, God adores cooing.

"Fill my heart with joy when their grain and new wine abound." Psalm 4:7 (NIV)

Personal Reflection:

What is your most significant cause of tension, and what is one thing you can do to help alleviate the stress?

Twenty-Four

PSALMS FOR THANKFUL MOMS

Lisa's Reflection

I am extremely grateful that mommas aren't issued report cards, for I fear I would have earned my fair share of D's and F's, possibly even some incompletes. Yet with dismal grades like these, my kids would still love me unconditionally.

Isn't that an amazing feat? Where else in the world can you mess up on a continual basis and not risk being fired or rejected? Not many places, other than being with God, of course.

I never asked my kids if they were thankful for me. It seemed a self-serving question until the day they each moved out and I decided to ask it, and they answered. Their responses indelibly changed my life on the spot.

They gave me concrete examples of their thankfulness. No one mentioned Disneyland vacations or Hanukkah gifts. Instead, rug picnics and running in the rain made the top spots.

I can't write more about their recollections without crying.

So thank you, God, for gifting me with the most glorious of blessings. I may not always appear thankful, but I am. I truly am.

I don't even have the words to properly describe the magnitude of my thankfulness.

Sometimes in the chaos and craziness of my motherhood moments, I lose my perspective, criticize and complain, and sometimes (I'm embarrassed to admit this) I even whine.

Please know that in the quietest of moments when I can hear your whispers, I'm overwhelmed with thankfulness beyond all rhyme and reason.

I know that I will feel this way now and for all the days of my life. I thought it wouldn't hurt to make sure you knew this to be my truth.

"Give thanks to the LORD, for He is good his love endures forever." Psalm 118:1 (NIV)

Shelby's Reflection

As moms, we have so much to be thankful for each day. Although never our intent, we can be lulled into complacency because of our busyness and forget to take the time to praise God with appreciation and gratitude.

Other times, giving thanks seems contrary and impossible because we are knee-deep in situations of pain, fear, worry, disappointment, anger, or sadness.

God reminds me on the regular how praising Him in the storm is a greater act of faith and devotion than shouting out with joy when life is great.

I struggle with this big time. Mostly because when I am consumed by what hurts, all I can muster is crying out for relief. In all my begging I forget the ways God's worked things out in the past, how many times He's delivered me and those I love. I even forget the number of ways He answers prayers, works His wonder for the greater good.

The Psalms are full of scripture verses about giving thanks to God. For today's reflection, I thought we could read through them with a bent towards our motherhood journey—the struggles and the joys—as a reminder of how important it is for us to give thanks and praise.

All verses are from NLT, emphasis mine:

"Make thankfulness your ***motherly*** *sacrifice to God, and keep the vows you made to the Most High."* Psalm 50:14

"Enter ***each morning*** *with thanksgiving; go into* ***every situation with your child*** *with praise. Give thanks to him and praise his name* ***for every instance...especially those that ruffle your feathers, worry you sick, leave you confused.****"* Psalm 100:4

"Sing a song of thanksgiving and tell ***your children*** *of all God's wonders* ***being worked out in your life and theirs.****"* Psalm 26:7

"The Lord is my strength and shield ***throughout my mothering journey.*** *I* ***entrust my kids to*** *him with all my heart. He helps me* ***make wise decisions, endure heartache, overcome my fears, mother with love and patience****, and my heart is filled with joy. I burst out in songs of thanksgiving."* Psalm 28:7

"Then I will praise God's name ***for the gift of my children*** *with singing, and I will honor him with thanksgiving."* Psalm 69:30

"I will offer you ***my time, energy, nurturing, loving, consoling, caring, teaching, and enduring as*** *a sacrifice of thanksgiving and call on the name of the LORD."* Psalm 116:17

"...that I might sing praises to you and not be silent. O LORD, my God, I will give you thanks ***for every step of my mothering journey; grateful for the precious moments AND the times of deep suffering****, forever!"* Psalm 30:12

"But giving thanks ***when nothing makes sense, you are ready to give up, you doubt I am working out everything for good, you see your children faltering*** *is a sacrifice that truly honors me. If you keep to my path, I will reveal to you the salvation of God."* Psalm 50:23

"I will fulfill my vows to you, O God, and will offer a sacrifice of thanks for your help ***in raising my kids as best I can.****"* Psalm 56:12

"It is good to give thanks to the Lord ***especially when I'm worried sick, angry, frustrated, hurt, confused, feel rejected****, and to sing praises to the Most High."* Psalm 92:1

"Praise the LORD! Give thanks to the LORD, for he is good ***even when life seems bad****! His faithful love endures forever—****a love beyond my comprehension and greater than I feel for my own children.****"* Psalm 106:1

"Give thanks to him who alone does mighty miracles, ***none more amazing than giving me the gift of loving and raising a child and the indescribable blessing of being loved in return.*** *His faithful love endures forever."* Psalm 136:4

Amen.

Personal Reflection:

Start a gratitude journal by writing down five things you are thankful for each night before bed. Observe your emotions, and see if they begin to change

Twenty-Five

PSALMS FOR THREATENED MOMS

Shelby's Reflection

Our kids are growing up in a world full of hostility, dangers, violence, and temptations—all of which impact their well-being. It's impossible to quantify the number and magnitude of evils competing for our kids' souls—each one a threat to the health, safety, and security of the generations below us. How do we manage all that jeopardizes the potential of our children having a hope-filled, long-lasting, peaceful future?

It's undoubtedly impossible and unreasonable to fight a war against every enemy. We can pray for sure, trusting God's going to win the final battle. But what if we pick one area threatening their livelihood and make a mindful, momma bear decision to do something about it? I've spent a lot of years barking up trees and kicking tires about the casualties of society: drug crisis, porn epidemic, trafficking, bullying, and violence. To be fair, my husband and I have invested years in various ministries trying to make a small difference.

I think the challenge for all of us as mothers is to go big on one issue we feel super passionate about. Real change happens with grassroots involvement, and that's our jam. We are in the trenches of motherhood and see first-hand what our kids are dealing with: the pain, struggle, weariness, emptiness, and confusion from this fast-paced, insensitive, and broken world.

If we couple a concerted effort to engage a threat with confident pleas to God for guidance and protection, then we can trust in His ability to stand with our kids and us in the battle against evil.

"Listen and help, O God.
I'm reduced to a whine
And a whimper, obsessed
with feelings of doomsday.
Don't let them find (our children)—
the conspirators out to get (them),
Using their tongues as weapons,
flinging poison words,
poison-tipped arrow-words.
They shoot from ambush,
shoot without warning,
not caring who they hit.
They keep fit doing calisthenics
of evil purpose,
They keep lists of the traps
they've secretly set." Psalm 64:1-5 (MSG, emphasis mine)

Lisa's Reflection

We're carousing on the playground carousel. I prance around the park, swing to slide, slide to swing, gently coaxing my children into carefree corners. Applauding heights reached and successful ground landings, joining in the raucous hoots and hollers like the best of play dates.

I make gentle demands for potty breaks at regular intervals.

Like all mommas, I am a gentle soul.

Until I sense danger in the form of a stranger lurking, gawking by the seesaw.

I stand at ATTENTION, every fiber of my momma being on RED ALERT.

I summon my babies quickly, expertly swooping them up

and shooing them out of harm's way in ONE motion.

They balk a bit as I reassure them.

As a momma, I am mostly a gentle soul.

Until I feel THREATENED.

When it comes to my children, all bets are off!

Mommas possess Incredible Hulk capabilities. It's part of our DNA.

We will overpower and take down the enemy, risking our own lives to ensure the safety of our babies.

Once the threat has been removed, we return to being gentle souls who push swings and wipe runny noses. All while cherishing our status as our children's favorite playmate.

Don't mess with the momma.

"In the LORD I take refuge. How then can you say to me: "Flee like a bird to your mountain!" Psalm 11:1 (NIV)

Personal Reflection:

What is one threat against your child/family you can go big on and make a difference right now?

Twenty-Six
PSALMS FOR TIRED MOMS

Lisa's Reflection

Dear God,

I do not have an ounce of energy left within me.

I think you may have over-estimated my mom stamina and endurance.

I heard a rumor that we don't get more than we can handle, yet is it possible you might have overlooked the fact that I am one of the weak ones?

I don't feel fit for this job.

I'm not any good at it.

I'm not feeling it if you know what I mean.

I can dabble in the fun parts like Play-Doh for a few minutes here and Legos a few minutes there.

It's the rest of the stuff before, after, and in between that has brought me to my knees.

They all need me, God, and I am spent.

I don't know where to summon up anything more than I have, and it's NOT ENOUGH!

You ask how I know it's not enough?

Is that the question of the day?

Hear my tone, my attitude, my impatience?

They hear it and see it too, and I can't make it go away.

I try to hide my frustrations and disappointment, and I

know they feel it. It's their unhealed boo-boo that grows a scab and then bleeds all over again. I say I am sorry and they say it's okay. It's NOT OKAY!

I'm a dismal failure at this mom gig.

I need to crawl into a hole and disappear and come out when I am feeling capable. That could be a long time.

I'm tired, God.

Not of them. I love my kids more than life itself.

I'm tired of I don't know what.

If you know, could you please shed some light for me?

And please don't lead me anywhere to find the answer myself.

I would appreciate a little help on this one. Not wanting to sound desperate here, but I am in no mood to search and discover.

I am tired, God.

I am in over my head.

I love them with every ounce of my being. I don't think it's enough. Help me will you, God, please? Where is the source of strength I am seeking?

I am a mother.

I am tired.

And while venting, I figured out the answer to my question. The source of my strength can be found in the way my children look at me. Through their lens, I am everything as you are to me.

My tired is their blessing.

"But as for me, I am poor and needy; may the LORD think of me. You are my help and my deliverer; you are my God, do not delay." Psalm 40:17 (NIV)

Shelby's Reflection

Life is exhausting. Dot at the end of a sentence.

Raising kids is only a partial reason. We still have jobs, community/volunteer commitments, family å la carte activities, church, and a massive to-do list of never-ending priorities for maintaining and managing everything else. Somewhere in the midst of all that, we are also entrusted to ensure the health, safety, well-being, protection, and Franklin Planning of our kids for 18 years and counting.

So, yes, we are tired.

Being tired is super inconvenient since the sun appears to be rising and setting at a more blistering pace than ever before due to all the distractions in our current world. Before we finish our second yawn on Monday morning, it's time for bed on Friday. When will we ever catch up on needed zzzzs? Is sleep even possible in the mishmash of motherhood?

God for sure created moms with some kind of inherent caffeine gene or extra twist of stamina DNA because it's not humanly possible for one person to function on the amount of rest most moms get. Yet, somehow we keep going even when we have an infant or several children.

Like robots, we stiff leg ourselves along, one heavy clod after another, while physical, mental, emotional, and spiritual exhaustion pushes down our eyelids and sinks into our bones. Not only are we feeding, cleaning, molding, teaching, transporting, comforting, and every '*ing*' imaginable for our kids, we are also in a perpetual state of flight or fight, scanning the horizon for threats in every direction.

While I'm 100% thankful for God instilling the superhuman trait in us moms, I don't mind asking Him for a bit of extra blessing:

ME: Any chance you can give us the gift of feeling rested one day a week? Two would be fantastic, but I don't want to beg. I get you already gave us some real scripture encouragement for when we're feeling tired—which sounds lovely on paper by the way—but how about a solution for some real rest because we're real exhausted?

GOD: Be still, and know that I am God.

ME: I KNEW you were going to say that!

Ugh. Why does God always have to be right?!

"Have compassion on me, LORD, for I am weak. Heal me, LORD, for my bones are in agony." Psalm 6:2 (NLT)

Personal Reflection:
What will you do to take care of 'you' and rest this week?

Twenty-Seven
PSALMS FOR TRAPPED MOMS

Lisa and I did a short Q&A on feeling trapped as a mom. Here are our answers to the same questions.

Shelby's Reflection

1. **Have you ever felt trapped as a mom, and if so, in what way?**

Absolutely. Having three kids in 3 ½ years will do that to you. My husband worked long hours and traveled quite a bit for his job. At one point I didn't think there was any end in sight to my exhaustion or splintered nerves from not getting a break. Depression set in, and I really felt trapped, in my own body and in the mundane.

Then, when my kids moved into stages of more independence, I felt trapped because of the loss of control. I was stuck in worry and fear. During times of intense discord, I felt trapped in mom guilt—a vicious cycle of blaming myself for every poor choice and bad decision by my kid and every poor reaction and lousy way of handling the situation by me.

2. **What did you do to fix the situation or change your mindset? How did God help?**

Prayer, Godly friends, counsel, and an incredibly loving and supportive husband who helped me change my mindset and appreciate motherhood as a sum of many moving parts, both joyful and challenging—each a gift. Our kids grow up at the speed of light; every second matters. One of the most powerful scriptures to meditate upon is this: *"I am praying to you because I know you will answer, O God. Bend down and listen as I pray."* Psalm 17:6 (NLT)

My husband and I also got involved in Life Teen Ministry when our kids were in grade school, which proved to be an invaluable experience. Immersing ourselves in teen culture and hearing their real struggles, especially parental conflict and communication issues, helped us better parent when our kids became teens. The experience gave us more resolve to face our worries, doubts, and fears.

3. **Looking back, what would you do differently to avoid putting yourself in a similar situation, whether emotional or physical?**

Oh, how I would love to have a do-over in so many areas. I regret all the missed opportunities from allowing myself to feel so overwhelmed and consumed by worry and fear. I would have spent more time with empty nest moms. My outlook from this place is drastically different than when I was in the trenches—which makes perfect sense because I've matured, evolved, survived, overcome, and endured. I think, as a young mom, I could have handled the challenges and adversity much better had I found some mentors who had already weathered the storms and had a full-circle perspective.

I also would face my demons sooner. My mental health was a wreck for a long time. I tried to pray away and guilt away my weaknesses and shortcomings on my own when counseling was what I desperately needed. An enormous amount of pain from a broken past bled into my marriage and interactions with my kids for too many years—although I had no idea this was the root of my struggle until I finally sought help. My kids were 12, 10, and 8 by then.

4. **What advice do you have for young moms who feel trapped?**

Communicate, communicate, communicate—with your spouse, your family, your friends. Ask for help, for relief when you feel stuck in fear, worry, or insanity from the chaos. It's normal to feel trapped; you're not alone, and authenticity heals. Take care of yourself. When you feel lost, out of control, empty, or depressed, seek help. Work on you. We need to be healthy to raise healthy kids. We need to pray, mommas. Pray for strength, guidance, and an ability to trust that God's got this. He's got all of it. We just need to surrender as best we can and let God do what God does best in us and through us.

Lisa's Reflection

1. **Have you felt trapped as a mom, and if so, in what way?**

There were times, in fact too numerous to count, when I felt desperate to leave the room and in some instances the house. I'm surprised when I look back on these times that I didn't cave in. I craved my sanity and wanted to take a deep breath and regroup. It happened most often when no one was listening to me, which as we mommas know, occurs on a daily if not minute-by-minute basis.

When it seemed like the household was moving in reverse, I sometimes felt close to a ledge. I was convinced that Alice and the Looking Glass were mere feet away from where I stood. It took realizing that I was the grown-up in the room, the one responsible for these little lives, to take a figurative step back and regain my perspective.

2. **What did you do to fix the situation or change your mindset? How did God help?**

More often than not, the situation remedied itself with a little humor and the most patience I could muster. Through tantrums that reached the peak on the Richter scale, to everyone's needs colliding at once, I found a few simple tricks that resulted in temporary truces and the restoration of my sanity:

a. I would sing at the top of my lungs, which was really yelling in disguise. It made the kids stop in midstream whatever they were doing and stare at me. Then they laughed. It was contagious. Then I laughed. Calm returned to the home front.

b. I would lie down on the living room rug and encourage the kids to tickle me until I yelled for mercy. Their giggles charmed me, their touch melted me, and I was reminded what I loved about being a momma in the first place.

c. I would explain to the kids (in an age-appropriate way) that Mommy was having a hard day and I needed their help. The success rate for this strategy over 20 years? Close to 100%. And it's my best-kept secret weapon. To this day I use it on the big kids and the hubby.

God helped by letting me discover all of this on my own. I was mystified back then why He didn't provide direct answers. Then I realized I already had the answers and He trusted me to find them.

"The Lord is close to all who call on him, yes, to all who call on him in truth." Psalm 145:18 (NLT)

3. **Looking back, what would you do differently to avoid putting yourself in a similar situation, whether emotional or physical?**

I would have reached out to a family member, a friend, or clergy and sought their help. I didn't for fear of being judged a failure by them and more importantly, myself. Motherhood is not meant to be performed solo.

On the kibbutz' in Israel and in many species of the animal kingdom, a sisterhood of women raises the young. All Mommas need someone to be there for them in their best of days and their worst. If I had shared my thoughts of feeling trapped, I don't believe they would have escalated to the point where I wished to escape.

And at other specific times when being overwhelmed threatened to consume me, I sought professional intervention which, as a mental health professional myself, I recommend highly.

4. **What advice do you have for young moms who feel trapped?**

SPEAK UP! SPEAK OUT! Do it loud. Do it often. Never hold your feelings inside. Find an older momma, someone who has already walked a similar journey who will understand and hear you. It's important to know you're never alone. Allow another momma the chance to take you under her wing and provide encouragement and most of all, *hope*. It'll be good for both of you.

Having someone you can share with who's been there and overcome is like having your own personal cheerleader to guide you. She's also a perfect choice for a babysitter so new Momma can grab a cup of coffee in peace.

On a lighter note, put clean underwear on every day. You may not shower for three or four days, but fresh undies make you feel somewhat human. Otherwise, you'll feel like a contestant on Naked and Afraid.

Personal Reflection:

How would you answer these same questions?

Twenty-Eight

PSALMS FOR UNMOTIVATED MOMS

Lisa's Reflection

I am having one of those days.

No, let me be more honest and straightforward.

I've been having these days of late where I don't have the motivation to go beyond the basic daily routine.

The kid's alarm clocks ring.

I encourage wake-ups.

I force wake-ups.

Clothes are picked out.

Different clothes are picked out.

Hair is brushed through tangles and tears.

More tears accompanied by whimpers.

Whimpers escalating to screams when the knots resist.

Two bites of toast with Nutella.

Fights about taking two more bites.

Plates pushed aside.

Voices raised in protest (mine primarily).

Lunch boxes were packed the night before.

Lunch boxes missing dry ice.

Dry ice missing in freezer.

Bus at curb.

Tousled hair.

Quick air kisses (though I secretly wished for lip locks).

Curbside waves.

Four eyes ignoring the momma.
Bus pulls away.
Bed beckons.
Baby cries.
Momma needs an infusion of something.
God, excuse me, are you there?

"Take delight in the LORD, and he will give you the desires of your heart." Psalm 37:4 (NIV)

Shelby's Reflection

Have you ever seen one of those motivational posters? You know like the rock climber hanging off a cliff with a big, bold "PERSEVERANCE" message underneath? Or the serene beach scene with a colorful sunset that says "ATTITUDE"?

Yeah. Those are lovely. But where are the motivational posters for moms? Because the glorious nature scenes just aren't capturing the real and raw of everyday monotony.

Where are the posters with a vibrant photo of a kitchen with unclean dishes flowing like lava out of the sink onto counters, with an all caps "RESILIENCE" underneath? Or a panoramic of a living room littered with lone socks, smashed grapes, Legos, spilled sippy cups, random game pieces, and an array of books with the caption: "CLOSE YOUR EYES AND IMAGINE…anything else"? How about a full wall mural of dirty laundry with the word "GOALS" sprawled across the middle in a massive font?

Would the humor motivate us enough to want to do the things, day in and day out? Doubtful. Because I remember those days, and my toes still curl in my shoes when reminiscing.

The 'all things mom' dictionary says this about housework: mundane, endless, monotonous, drab; a necessary inevitability. "Domestic drudgery conjures up a sense of extraordinary fulfillment," said no one ever.

Finding purpose and meaning in the boring and menial can feel almost counterproductive. Then God says this: *"So here's what I want you to do, God helping you: Take your everyday, ordinary life—your sleeping, eating, going-to-work, and walking-around life—and place it before God as an offering. Embracing what God does for you is the best thing you can do for him."* Romans 12:1 (MSG)

I'm not convinced God said this, because, well, Paul said this. But Paul was not a mother inundated with housework and nerve-frying responsibilities. Of this I am convinced—which was my argument to God for years. Then God wormed His way into my whines (but I try to keep Him out of my wines). He helped me find peaceful asylum by re-purposing relentless household duties into a life lesson for building a strong work ethic in my children.

Our family may have had the most detailed and thought-out chore chart of all time. Just ask my kids. The elaborate spreadsheet was the talk of every guest who visited. For real. Chores alternated by kid, by week, by activity. Equal agony, across the board, on repeat. The rewards were great. My to-do list of all things boring shrunk and the kids learned how to serve and contribute—even if they weren't always thrilled.

Despite allocating certain chores, our kids can't help us with everything, nor motivate us to do the agonizing mundane. So, what do we do? I learned to consider the greater reward of what we do as mommas in the trenches.

The truth is, none of the boring and monotonous would exist without the blessing of raising kiddos in the first place. While we may never whistle with glee over doing dishes, washing clothes, cleaning toilets, or filling out school paperwork, we can shift our focus to the payoff: a rich life of raising kids that is full of love and eternal purpose. This truth adds gourmet chocolate sauce and sprinkles to the vanilla of everyday living.

"Children are a heritage from the LORD, offspring a reward from him. Like arrows in the hands of a warrior are children born in one's youth. Blessed is the man whose quiver is full of them." Psalm 127:3-5 (NIV)

Personal Reflection:

Reflect on the rewards of God's faithfulness as you love and steward your children.

Twenty-Nine

PSALMS FOR VULNERABLE MOMS

Shelby's Reflection

Dear God,

You gifted me with the miracle of motherhood three times over. My two sons and daughter are healthy by most standards and are all living life large on love and blessings. My marriage is healthy because I have an incredible spouse who loves, serves, and provides selflessly. We share good health and have all we need and then some, because of your grace and provision.

But here's the thing: I still struggle with all kinds of emotions and strongholds as a mom, even though so many things about my life are going right. Since you are God, you know I'm insecure, a worrier, and a fear monger. You see me battle with mom guilt and understand how I long to do certain things better. I've made tons of mistakes over the years and still have flaws in need of Holy tinkering.

This truth is why my heart hurts for moms who struggle with these same universal vulnerabilities but also carry the added weight of other areas in their life not going so right:

- Single moms who are pulling the weight of two parents emotionally, physically, financially, and spiritually. They don't have the holistic support of a loving spouse. I can't imagine how vulnerable they feel about making ends meet, having the emotional stamina to deal with raising children alone. Please take extra care of them, Lord. Help the rest of us moms lean in and love them, respect what they are going through, and help where we can.

- Divorced moms struggling with rejection, abandonment, and shame. I don't walk in their shoes, Lord, but help me and others understand the vulnerability they carry related to security and self-love so we can show more tenderness and compassion.
- Widowed moms, moms who've lost a child, moms who've lost a parent or loved one and now wrestle with devastating loss. Lord, I can't find words. Their vulnerability spans a depth I can't begin to fathom. Only you know their pain firsthand. So please help us love them deeply by just being there—letting them know we see them and they matter. Remind us to say extra prayers for their broken hearts.
- Sick moms and moms caring for spouses, children, and aging parents with health issues of any kind. The vulnerability centered around worry, fear, and overall unsettledness over what each day will bring is beyond measure for these moms. Help the rest of us respect their vulnerability by not taking our health for granted and also letting them know we care and are willing to help.

Lord, you know there are many more examples of moms carrying the extra weight of the world on their backs, causing their vulnerability levels to be sky high. We don't even know who these moms are half the time because they hide their wounds and scars. So please help us to remember every mom has a story, to be mindful and loving at all times, and to have compassion. Help us avoid the mom foul of shallow judgments, harsh criticisms, and rejection based on ignorance—not just towards others, but towards ourselves as well.

Help us love, Lord.

"Let your compassion come to me that I may live, for your law is my delight." Psalm 119:77 (NIV)

Lisa's Reflection

It's hard to admit feeling vulnerable when you're a mom.

Kids are supposed to feel vulnerable. It comes with the territory.

It's understood. It's accepted.

Moms are the warriors staving off danger and warding off harm 24/7. We're in the protecting our kids business.

Then who protects the momma when she is feeling vulnerable?

The answer? The momma.

We are expected to function on full throttle, no matter how vulnerable we might be on any given day. No one really wants to hear our woes. So what do mommas do? We lift ourselves up by the proverbial bootstraps, suck it up and provide, protect and persevere.

Not fair! Mommas need an outlet when they feel weakened and insecure. A "Vulnerability Hotline"? A "Mommas experiencing Vulnerability" counseling group?

How about starting with the truth and branching out from there?

Mommas need to be told and reassured that vulnerability also comes with our territory.

We can't help ourselves if we are forced to hide our vulnerability like we do Easter eggs.

It has to be okay to admit we're feeling vulnerable.

Once one momma stands up and says it out loud, then the next momma hears it and realizes it's all right to join the chorus.

Before long, a tribe of extraordinary women has formed an outer circle around its most vulnerable members.

The outer circle changes with need and circumstance.

Let's all start there, admitting we're vulnerable—out loud, with dignity and grace. No shame. No judgment.

I'll start.

"I'm Lisa. I'm going through a very vulnerable time in my life. I sure could use a friend."

"Create in me a clean heart, O God, and renew a steadfast spirit within me." Psalm 51:10 (NIV)

Personal Reflection:

Who provides a safe space for you to open up and share your heart? Will you?

Thirty
PSALMS FOR WORRIED MOMS

Lisa's Reflection

What happens *if*? That universal nagging question that takes up more space in our psyche than anything else when it comes to our children: Mom worry. Mom and worry. One does not exist without the other. And they do not co-exist harmoniously. We worry excessively, and it takes us away from pretty much everything!

What happens if the bus for the school trip does not have a bathroom on board and the teacher forgets to remind my daughter to use the one in her classroom before they leave?

What happens if she gets motion sickness and throws up? She didn't bring a change of clothes with her.

What happens if she feeds the baby zoo animals and they have a disease?

What happens if she doesn't have enough money to buy a zoo souvenir for me?

What happens if her best friend wants to change seats on the way home and excludes her?

These are simple worries over a little basic trip to the animal petting zoo. Think about how the worries increase exponentially with age (not the mom's) when our children are out in the world fending for themselves, and we have to give up our constant desire to manipulate and interfere with the outcomes.

Since it would be inappropriate to recommend wine to subdue our worries, what else works?

For starters, talking to women who blazed the trail before us and survived the worry trenches is a glorious beginning.

It's reassuring to know that a) we're not alone in our excessive worry and b) we can make it through at least high school graduation with guidance from a momma mentor (college worry is a whole different breed).

This symbiotic relationship of worried moms receiving wisdom and encouragement from "been there worried moms" works so efficiently it should be recommended in all parenting manuals.

In truth, it appears that worry is part of the maternal make-up.

We've been engaged in this behavior since the beginning of time, and I imagine we will continue to function as worry-warts until the end of time.

Therefore, we ought to surround ourselves with the elder and more experienced in the sisterhood so they can offer their teachings and life lessons.

And then there's God.

I know that handing our worries over to God constitutes the best of answers.

Plus, each one of us has discovered ways that work pretty effectively in conjunction with God's efforts.

Can you share what you've discovered with your tribe, so they are equipped for whatever worry-laden situation they face tomorrow?

"God, you are my light and my salvation, whom shall I fear? You are the strength of my life, of whom shall I be afraid?" Psalm 27:1 (NIV)

Shelby's Reflection

Pretty sure I've earned a doctorate in all things worry after 25 years of the mom thing. No one's mailed me a diploma, but my credentials could fill up the Library of Congress. Worry debilitates me on the regular, a constant sidekick that tangles my emotions and robs me of sleep. Our relationship steeps in toxicity, which is why I may not be the best person to write about how to battle such a superpower. I'm confident many of you could spin some much-needed wisdom *my way*. But what I can offer is how I've taken infant steps towards overcoming my fret addiction.

The most important realization for me was coming to understand how much time I spend in my head. Relentless ruminating over worst-case scenarios became one of my hobbies over the years. The thing is, all the narrative writing in my mind was illusionary at best. We make stuff up as we go, don't we? Imagination is wonderful for Walt Disney movies, but not so much when we use creativity to project doomsday plot lines.

I've learned that the first step to staying out of the thing between our ears is to make a mindful effort to spend more time in our heart. The way I do this is by getting quiet and taking a trip down memory lane. When we look back and search for examples of how God's worked things out in the past, the worry tends to dissipate under the proof of answered prayer. Trust and surrender come easier in light of God's past protection, healing, guidance, mercy, etc. We soon realize almost all of our *what ifs* never come to fruition, which means our vexing is a waste of valuable time and energy.

While I can't claim ownership to this phrase, putting into practice a trip down memory lane is choosing to *turn worry into worship*. I heard a pastor share this concept during a sermon at a Chris Tomlin concert and haven't been able to shake the power of his words ever since. In fact, every morning at 8am, my iPhone sends me a notification to "turn my worry into worship" as a reminder to be grateful for what God's already done and to praise Him for what He promises to do going forward.

"Be still in the presence of the LORD, and wait patiently for him to act. Don't worry about evil people who prosper or fret about their wicked schemes." Psalm 37:7 (NLT)

Personal Reflection:

What areas of your life would you benefit from turning your worry into worship?

Thirty-One
PSALMS FOR WORSHIPFUL MOMS

Shelby's Reflection

So, I am a worship music junkie in every Hillsong United way, not to mention a super fan of a long list of other favorite praise and worship stars including Kari Jobe, Casting Crowns, Chris Tomlin, and Lauren Daigle. Something about the build-up in the musical masterpieces they sing fills every nook and cranny of my being. When Hillsong's, *Of Dirt & Grace: Live from the Land* released, I began a listening frenzy that cast me into a sea of comatose wonder. When I found out the fun fact about the album being recorded and filmed in the Holy Land—raw and uncut compilations performed in locations where Jesus walked—I died. This after I cried. For days. The mere thought of people singing a song on the hillside where Jesus gave His Sermon on the Mount and in a boat floating on the same water upon which He walked slayed me. I was so moved, I bought the live album video and sat with my husband and sob- watched every song, start to finish. True story.

I'm not dramatic. But I do love me some worship music.

Which brings me to the point of this last reflection: worship music is magic. The lyrics have a way of pixie dusting our mom hearts just when we need a reprieve from our circumstances. Here are some suggestions for dealing with your mom emotions using Hillsong United worship songs, all from the *Of Dirt & Grace* album:

1. When you are peeved to no end, raging like a crazy people, try playing *Here Now (Madness)*, filmed and recorded on the doorstep of the Garden Tomb right below where many believe Golgotha was, you cannot stay mad. Seriously.

2. When you are desperate beyond measure, worried sick, afraid of all the *what ifs* and *what nows,* listen to *Oceans (Where Feet May Fail),* recorded on the Sea of Galilee. If the karma of Peter walking on water to meet Jesus can't boost your trust meter, nothing will. Believe me when I tell you, this song saved my life four years ago. My mom heart was thrown overboard in a huge way, and then God spun this masterpiece into my airwaves. I've officially broken Spotify ten times from overplaying the song. Not really. But this song really is my ringtone on my iPhone.

3. When mom guilt, shame, or remorse of any kind sends you into a deep dive, listen to *When I Lost My Heart to You (Hallelujah),* recorded in the dark of night with the Sea of Galilee and Tiberius as a backdrop. Nothing like meeting Jesus in the stillness and trusting in His magnificent love to lessen your self-bashing and refresh your soul.

When it comes to all things motherhood, worship and praise are like counting to ten or taking a mental health timeout in the bathroom. It's hard to stay stuck in the muck when we focus on God and His Glory. Loving on Him, remembering His promises, and pouring out our hearts always leads to finding magnificent Grace in the mishmash of all things.

"Open your mouth and taste, open your eyes and see how good God is. Blessed are you who run to him." Psalm 34:8 (MSG)

Lisa's Reflection

I don't want my kids to worship me.

I am a mere mortal mother whose shortcomings most notably outweigh my talents on chaotic school mornings when I manage to hand out burnt toast for breakfast and call it a morning.

I don't think I want my kids to worship other kids either.

Kids are kids, which makes them equal partners in the crime of being able to drive mommas crazy!

Then there are the glorious teachers and coaches and sports heroes that will come across our children and shape and mold and mentor.

I do not want them to worship those fabulous folks either.

I want them to respect them and speak honorably about them, but worship need not play a role.

What do I want my kids to do?

I want them to listen and watch me being worshipful in my words and daily deeds, knowing God is in attendance.

I want them to see me trying to do my best in the eyes of God, and when I fall short, pick myself up and start where I left off, still praising and still worshipful. God appreciates when we worship Him whether we're in pajamas and not showered for three days or sneaking in prayers of gratitude between soccer mom carpools. Whether we're apologizing to our kids for letting a few curse words slip out when we stepped on a Lego barefoot, or when we're kneeling at the side of our kids' beds teaching them how to worship and thank God before and after the 1500 potty breaks, boogeyman under the sheet checks, and requests for water.

I don't want my kids to worship me. Maybe a little bit here and there. Hopefully, God won't mind!

"Let everything that has breath praise the LORD. Praise the LORD." Psalm 150:6 (NIV)

Personal Reflection:

How easy is it to praise and worship God in times of struggle and heartache?

More About Shelby

Shelby is a sarcasm aficionado and sappy soul whisperer who fell in love with the man of her dreams at first sight. Soon after, she fell hard for Jesus after witnessing her hubby's beautiful faith in action. Together, John and Shelby have packed in 25 years of togetherness built on a foundation of LOVE. John will tell you his time with Shelby has been the best 16 years of his life.

Their three amazing kiddos filled their nest with laughter and love for over two decades. But to be fair, the years also included plenty of chaos, not to mention more tough stuff than should be legal. At least that's the complaint Shelby's had with God over the years.

Now Shelby sits alone in her empty abyss and writes words about her love for Jesus and all she's learned and had to unlearn along the journey of marriage and motherhood. You can find her musings on her blog at shelbyspear.com as well as in print at *Guideposts*. She's known as the first writer in the history of the publication to share a story about getting a tattoo—a transformational moment shared with her teenage daughter.

Online, Shelby is a frequent contributor to *Her View From Home, For Every Mom, Today Show,* and many other online sites. She just finished up her memoir about how Jesus uses everyday life to unmask, heal, and free your authentic self.

More About Lisa

Lisa is excited to be entering a new frontier in her life; meeting the eligibility requirement for Dunkin' Donuts senior discount. Because she's now a 'biddy,' she lives in the same attire as new Mommas: t-shirts and sweats for daily living and extravagant affairs.

She's ready to pursue a career in stand-up comedy if someone discovers she's funny. She's also ready to publish her children's book, *A Royal Mistake,* if someone discovers she's written it.

Lisa prays every day that the world becomes a more tolerant and accepting place. She hopes that each one of us will work towards making a lasting contribution to ensure this outcome.

When it's all said and done, Lisa's wish is that everyone walks with lightness, giggle easily, and land softly someday in the arms God.

Connect With Shelby and Lisa

For more info and resources from Shelby
shelbyspear.com

shelspear

shelspear

@shelspear

shelspear

For more info and resources from Lisa

lisa.leshaw.7

@LeshawLisa

Connect and share your thoughts about the book along with a picture using the hashtag #momfeelingsbook

28793538R10079

Made in the USA
Lexington, KY
21 January 2019